Self

MW01148976

Develop Good Habits.
Achieve Your Goals.

Jennifer Alison

Table of Contents

A Fresh Start

"Happiness is dependent on self-discipline. We are the biggest obstacles to our own happiness. It is much easier to do battle with society and with others than to fight our own nature."
Dennis Prager

Getting what you want out of life isn't always easy. In fact, the amount of self-discipline and determination it takes to provide us with personal gratification is outstanding. And that's not all we're after. Most of us also want career success and financial stability. We want to look good and feel great. We want to raise happy, healthy children. We want to be good citizens of the world. We want to live lives that we can be proud of, and we want the rewards we feel we deserve. At times, it can feel like life is a constant uphill battle. Time and time again, we fall short of our goals. Something always has to give. We get stuck in a rut. We feel hopeless and jaded by unfairness and defeat. We feel frustrated when we take stock of our lives. Most of us are able to motivate ourselves for short periods of time, but we may lose that determination when the going gets tough. We procrastinate, take the easy way out, or make constant excuses when we fail to reach our goals.

But each time we set goals that we never reach, it hurts us. Over time, as our unrealized dreams mount up, most of us lose some, if not all, of our lust for life. Getting caught in repetitive cycles of determination and defeat is taxing on the soul. It depresses your self-esteem and can leave you feeling empty and unsure of your true capabilities.

Take a moment to ask yourself:
How many times have you made a resolution that you didn't follow through with?
Have you often wanted to create lasting change in your life but have fallen short at the first or second hurdle?
Do you struggle to get going in the morning?
Do you have a hard time staying excited about a goal once you've started working toward it?

Do you give up easily?

Are you prone to making excuses when things don't go your way?

Do you lack organizational skills or the ability to manage your time effectively?

Are you surrounded by half finished projects?

Would you consider yourself to be a procrastinator?

Do your past moments of defeat make you doubt yourself?

Are you the type of person who really wants to change things in your life but no matter how much you try, things still remain the same?

There are so many aspects of our lives that rely on our ability to be disciplined with ourselves. Whether you want to live a healthier lifestyle or start a business, without self-discipline, things probably won't your way. You may find that you give up on your diet or change your mind about your business plans when things don't go to plan or when you realize just how much work you'll have to put in. Perhaps you become bored or disinterested before you even get into your stride. Maybe it seems easier to give up than facing the possibility of failure. But when things don't go our way, how can we make ourselves persevere? How can we trust ourselves to achieve anything if we don't know how to keep ourselves motivated? How can we feel confident enough to face our failures honestly, and continue pushing forward despite them?

We might start by accepting that there will always be some amount of unpredictability in our lives. We need to accept that for each of us, there will be obstacles and hardships that might get in the way of our progress. But we have to know deep in our cores that we can face these things head on. We need to prove to ourselves that we are unshakable. We have to believe that even if we get knocked back a few times, our goals are still achievable. Most importantly, we must learn how to recover from failure, and how to move past it. Without these vital skills, we may never reach our goals in life. We might watch opportunity pass us by more than a few times. We might be so afraid of failure that we continue living lives that are unfulfilling and unsatisfying.

Self-discipline can be either the thing that holds you back in life or the thing that propels you forward.

If you can't harness it, it will keep you rooted to the spot. If you take hold of it and use it to the best of your ability, it will guide you forward. This book will take that theory and encourage you to implement it into your life. It will take a *personal* approach to self-discipline. That is to say, it will not simply give you a few tips and tricks to help you stay on track; rather, it will help you get to the bottom of what has held you back from self-discipline and self-progression in the past, so that you can go into the future with a clear head and a brave heart. It will lead you through some simple self-reflection so that you can identify your strengths and weaknesses and use them as fuel for your fire. Your own personal experiences have provided you with resources and knowledge that can guide you to the life you want. With that knowledge, some invaluable practical skills, and the motivational approach laid out in this book, reaching your goals and being self-disciplined is entirely possible for anyone.

Change is rarely easy. The core of effective self-discipline is knowing what you truly desire and effectively measuring how much you're prepared to do to get it. You must be able to assess possibilities realistically and organize your life successfully. But there are many other things, on a deeper level, which may also affect your desired outcome. Your self-beliefs play a large part in your successes and failures. Your level of self-confidence will dictate the type of challenges you set for yourself. Your support system, your personal obstacles, virtually every part of your life will influence your ability to stick with something to the end. We all have habits that need to be retrained. We all have a home life and a work life that may impede on what we're trying to achieve. And there is always the inescapable possibility of failure looming over us every step along the way.

This book is going to provide you with the key to mastering self-discipline. It will cover all the basic principles of self-discipline as well as encouraging you to think about yourself and your life with a curious mind. It will guide you through realistic and effective goal setting and supply you with a world of practical skills that will help keep you on track. You will be encouraged to harness the dedication and confidence you need to get what you want out of life, as well as gaining some motivational insight on what to do when things don't go your way. You will also develop a foundation of self-reflection, which will help you to understand your own personal obstacles so that you can move forward and make a lasting change. This book is not just for the one goal you're toying with right now. Rather, it is one that will be with you for life, motivating you to keep reaching higher, and guiding you toward the life you want.

Take a moment right now to think about yourself and how your life has been up to this point. Think of this as your first exercise in self-discipline. Don't keep reading on or scan the book for what you *think* you really need. Don't take a break to go do the laundry or walk the dog. If you want to be more self-disciplined, start now!

Think about the goals you have set for yourself in the past.
Which goals have you achieved?
Which have you fallen short of?
Is there something you've tried to do many times in your life but still haven't quite accomplished it?
Can you identify a pattern in your life? For instance, do you run at your goals like a racehorse but give up before the race even starts?
Do you procrastinate or make excuses?
Are there some things that just seem impossible for you?
Do you have a hard time picking yourself up after a failure?

When doing this kind of self-reflection, it's important to be honest with yourself. Thinking this way is a vital part of learning self-discipline. Being able to realistically assess where things are going wrong can be tough, and it may even bring up some difficult emotions. But the more you understand about your thought patterns and behavior, the better equipped you will be to alter them. Everyone is different, and even though self-discipline is 100% possible no matter who you are, we all have our own quirks and habits that will need to be addressed on our own individual journeys. Being more aware of your personal challenges will be an immensely helpful resource for you to use as you move toward reaching your goals. Unfortunately, if we ignore our bad habits or constantly make excuses, rather than being able to accept blame when it's due, we are unlikely to get the things we want out of life. Our time on earth is limited. Do you want to spend yours gratified or dissatisfied? It really is that simple.

The fact is, if you've felt the need to buy this book then it shows that what you've been doing up to now just isn't working. So, it's time to make a change. It's time to learn how to get motivated and stay motivated no matter what it is that you're reaching for. So whether you want to save money, lose weight, get an education, set a good example for your children, finish a home renovation, or embark on a new career path, it's time to rewrite the way you approach challenges. Today, you're going to start something that you *will* finish. You're going to prove to yourself that you can do this.

"You are the one that possesses the keys to your being. You carry the passport to your own happiness."
Diane von Furstenberg

Reach Your Goals

"Failure will never overtake me if my determination to success is strong enough."
Og Mandino

When it comes to reaching our goals in life, we have to first think clearly and productively about what kind of goals we're actually setting for ourselves. Many times when we fall short of achieving what we want or we find ourselves giving up again and again, we can fall into patterns of beating ourselves up. Of course, you will need to identify the problem - you'll need to think about why you can't seem to get where you want to go - but a lot of times this kind of thinking can focus to heavily our own faults and flaws, which is not always productive. For some people, when faced with defeat, the aim might be to forget about the whole thing so that you don't end up feeling bad about it later. You might do everything you can to erase it from your memory completely, or you may come up with some excuses to make yourself feel better about it.

Others will use their failed attempt to put themselves down. These are all common coping mechanisms in the face of failure, but unfortunately they are unlikely to lead you to any higher knowledge. Thought cycles which center around negativity can lower your confidence and hit your self-esteem where it counts. And when it comes to maintaining motivation, you're going to need a great deal of confidence, resilience, and healthy self-beliefs. But don't worry if you're not quite there yet! These things may take time and patience but they possible for anyone. If you're one of the lucky ones who already has a strong sense of self and positive self-beliefs, congratulations, you've got a head start.

In order to identify what it is about self-discipline that you struggle with and to ensure a more promising road ahead, you've got to start at the beginning. Think about the last time you didn't get what you aimed to achieve.

What was your original goal?

Was it attainable?

Was it the type of thing you could've been better prepared for?

Did you have enough support in your life to get it done?

Did you have enough time to achieve it?

Were there any obstacles that were going to make things difficult no matter what? If so, did you think about them at the start and plan how you might overcome them?

This way of thinking; that is, exploring and planning for any possible obstacles that may get in your way *before* you jump into something head first; is what I like to call *active reflection*. It is the type of *productive thinking* that we need to be able to do when we're embarking on any new journey. Self-discipline isn't just about sticking with something when your mind starts to wander. It's about clearing the path before you even step onto it. It's about looking ahead so that you keep moving in the right direction when the road gets bumpy. Of all the ideas I will cover in this book, the most important thing you need in order to reach your target is the ability to set realistic goals for yourself. And unfortunately, this isn't always as straightforward as you may think.

Many of us set ourselves up for failure from the very start just by setting goals that we will never be able to achieve. We might try to do too much at once or underestimate how difficult the road ahead is going to be. We might take an overactive approach or a lazy one. The thing is, effective goal setting is a very individualized practice. Where one person may have all the time and energy in the world, others may have much less to give. Some people will have very little else going on in life, while others may be juggling kids, a career, hobbies, and an education all at once. More importantly, there are plenty of people in the world who just need to take smaller steps in order to reach their goals. We don't all move at the same pace. Some people are more prone to stress while others are almost always in a calm state of mind. None of us will have the same exact process and knowing this is should be a comfort, not something to worry about.

Most of us have things in our lives that are likely to get in our way, and it would be silly to ignore them. These things may be logistical concerns, emotional struggles, financial issues, or anything else life may throw your way. This is why some people find self-progression easy while others may find it extremely difficult. We all know someone who seems to have it all. They want to lose weight, and they do so with ease. They want a better job, and somehow they get one overnight. They want a husband and two children, and low and behold, three years later, they've got it all! But these are rare cases.

Most of us have personalities and circumstances that are a little more difficult to work with. Think about it. Someone with high self-esteem, a great support network, and a financially stable life is likely to find it easier to get what they want than someone who has been defeated a lot in life, who has a limited support network, and a small budget to work with. That just makes sense. But the good news is, whether you've already got most of the things you want out of life, or you were basically raised by wolves, you can still reach your personal goals! We all have to be willing to work with our own personal strengths and weaknesses, not fight against them.

So let's talk about effective goal setting. Start by thinking in baby steps. A lot of times, the reason we fall at the first hurdle is because we're thinking too big. It is wonderful, and *important*, to have big dreams, and I fully encourage you to hold onto yours because you really can achieve them, eventually. But when you're starting any sort of project, you will be far more successful if you keep your mind focused on smaller, more realistic targets. Setting small goals that lead up to your big goal means that you will have plenty of stops along the way to recharge your batteries. Plus, each time you reach one of your smaller targets, your self-esteem will benefit, your resolve will become stronger, you'll have something to celebrate, and you'll become more and more confident about eventually reaching that big goal. On the contrary, if you set your sights too high by reaching for something that's going to take a lot of time and energy to achieve - especially if it's unlikely to reap any rewards between now and then - you will naturally run out of steam long before you get there.

For example, if you're saving money to buy a house and all you can think about is the end goal, each deposit you make toward your house fund will begin to seem less and less significant. For many people, saving a large amount of money will take time and dedication, and if you're only able to save $200 each month when your goal is to save $20,000, it's going to be a long haul. So in order to keep yourself focused and excited about your future home, you've got to be able to feel good about the $200 you save each month, instead of feeling bad about $20,000 you haven't yet saved. It's all about mindset.

Are you likely to get your dream house any sooner just by changing your thinking? Probably not. But having a positive outlook will make the journey a lot more enjoyable, and ensure a higher likelihood of actually reaching your big goal. The reason for this is if you place too much focus on your big goal, you might give up on the smaller goals each month because they simply seem inconsequential in light of it. You might be inclined to save less each month or to use your savings for other, less important, things. If something is going to take years to save up for, why not splash out on a new TV and skip this month? Why not choose to take a vacation over the summer and start saving again in September? You have a choice between three options here. And that choice is between reaching your $20,000 goal feeling proud with a sense of accomplishment, reaching it feeling stressed out and exhausted, or not reaching it at all.

Try this one out for size. Let's say you need to lose 100 pounds. Your health is a factor, you want to look better, and you'd like to set a good example for your kids. You start eating well and moving more, and you're confident that you can lose around three pounds per week. At this slower, healthier rate, it's going to take you more than half a year to reach your big goal, and that time span can be pretty daunting when you're dieting. Are you more likely to stick to your diet by focusing on the 100 pound end goal or by keeping your mind focused on the three pound weekly goal? The fact is, losing three pounds may not be all that exciting, and it can feel insignificant in the grand scheme of things. But if you focus too much of your time thinking about the 100 pound goal, and you allow yourself become jaded by the seemingly insignificant three pound weigh-ins on the scale each week, you're more likely to give up entirely. Because, if your inner voice is constantly berating you for *only* losing three pounds each week, how likely are you to even get through the weekend without binging on junk food and wine?

Do you see what I mean by mindset? Smaller goals trick the mind into maintaining perspective and holding onto positivity as you gradually move toward bigger goals. So, whatever is it that you're working towards, think about some smaller goals that you can celebrate along the way. We need positive reinforcement in our lives. Human beings are relatively simple when it comes to this facet of our beings. Deep down, we are very much our child selves, in the way that our negative experiences cause poor self-beliefs and less positive experiences in general. For example, a child who is unhappy at school may be less likely to perform well, and may develop low self-esteem as a result. So too, as adults, an unhappy work environment is likely to cause us to produce subpar work. This is especially true for people who have a limited support network. The theory here is that by setting smaller goals, we are not only providing ourselves with more chances for success, but we are also reducing the possibility for failure. This, in turn, will help us to feel better about ourselves while making the things we want seem more attainable. Sometimes we have to be our own cheerleader in life, and that's not easy when it feels like your goal is impossible to achieve. Taking baby steps with plenty of breaks along the way, helps us keep our heads up and our eyes forward.

In tandem with this idea is the importance of setting *realistic* goals. Having hopes and dreams is immensely important and as I said earlier, I would never discourage you from dreaming big. However, there are times when goal setting can get a little out of control. There are times when we need to pare things down a bit. For instance, let's say it's New Year's Eve and you're ready to change your whole life at once. You make a resolution to give up smoking, eat better, have healthier relationships with your friends and family, go to the gym every day, stop drinking, plan a wedding, get a new job, and cure cancer all in the space of one year. This is obviously an exaggeration but my point is, that trying to change too much at once almost never works. And what's worse is that for each thing you don't achieve on that list, you will have to endure the pain and consequence of failure. Even when your intentions are good, you have to recognize when you're setting yourself up for a fall. Furthermore, setting even a single goal that's nearly impossible to achieve, won't do you any favors either.

Failure is not easy to recover from, and even when we're able to stomach it, it can have a way of chipping away at our self-esteem and challenging the way we view ourselves within the world around us. Simply starting the right way - that is, giving yourself a real chance to succeed by setting realistic goals - will have a dramatic effect on your journey toward getting what you want. So be honest and try to recognize if you're likely to put too much pressure on yourself. Pare it down to give yourself a better chance at succeeding.

The next thing you'll want to think about when you're setting goals is how they're going to fit into your life. If you've got a lot on your plate, you might need to think about giving yourself more time to reach your goal or letting go of something else while you're working toward it. Unfortunately, these things can be pretty tricky. Here's an example of what I mean. Let's say that I'm a self-employed single mother who goes to night school two days a week and loves getting outdoors with my dog on the weekends. Now let's say that what I want is to renovate my home and I want it done in no longer than one month's time. My income isn't too much to worry about but I don't have a lot of time on my hands. If I want to achieve this, while maintaining my life as it is, I'm going to have a really hard time and I'm not going to enjoy a minute of it. Because if I want to fit a month long renovation into my life as it stands, what I will have to do is either make myself and my family miserable or give up sleep for the month. I can't stop working because I need the money. I can't stop cooking dinner or helping my kids do their homework. I can't quit school because I need the qualification I'm working for and I've already paid for it. And getting out with the dog is my "me time". It's how I clear my head. So I need to figure out how I can keep juggling everything I have going on while fitting this renovation into my life without losing sleep. My options are to make my dog walks shorter or eliminate them completely, to ask or pay someone to help me, or to give myself more time to complete the home renovation. No matter what the circumstances are, sometimes something just has to give.

Taking time to think about things in depth before carving your goal into stone is wise. It not only means that you will be thinking more realistically, it also means that you will approach the whole thing with your wits about you. You're less likely to lose your head over setbacks if you anticipate them. You're less likely to become stressed out if you've made provisions for the rest of your life to fit into your goal plan. Prioritizing tasks isn't the most enjoyable part of goal setting but it does pay off in long run. Whether you decide to give yourself more time or you have to cut something out of your life for a while, you're more likely to continue on the right path if you've had a healthy degree of forethought leading up to times of change and challenge.

Another thing you'll want to keep in mind during the goal setting stage is what it is you really want. A lot of times we reach for things for the wrong reasons, our goals aren't quite what *we* want. Instead, we might be reaching for something that society tells us we should have. Or we do what our friends and family think is best for us instead of listening to our hearts. Being disciplined with yourself is pretty irrelevant if you don't even want what you're trying to get. It's hard to pave a path for ourselves when the world is telling us to do the opposite. The pressure placed on us by the media, the need to keep up with the Joneses, the competition we feel with our siblings… these are just a few of many things that can distort the way we view ourselves and our lives. We have to be able to judge ourselves by our own criteria. We have to be strong enough in our personal value system to live the life that makes us happy as individuals. There is no point reaching for something you don't want. That is not where satisfaction lies. It is infinitely easier to root for ourselves and to reach for better things, when we are reaching for the things we actually want. So if there's something that you've put a number of half-hearted attempts into, ask yourself if you really want it. If you don't, be kind enough to yourself to let it go.

Now, this next part might make your eyes roll, but bear with me! When it comes to setting goals and reaching them, you've got to believe in yourself. Sure, it's a cliché, but not without reason. Self-respect is not optional, it's a must-have.

You can't believe in yourself if you don't respect yourself. The good news is, if you don't already have it, self-respect is pretty easy to earn if you follow a few simple steps. If you're likely to put yourself down rather than building yourself up, you'll need to conquer and obliterate that habit. If you hear yourself being overly critical of yourself (aloud or in your head), stop it and reverse it. Instead of saying, "I could've done better" or "I'm a total failure", say "I did the best I could with what I had" or simply focus on what you *did* achieve. Every single time you accomplish something, no matter how insignificant it may seem, let yourself feel good about it. Give yourself a pat on the back. Even if it seems cheesy or silly, you've got to get into the habit of recognizing your strengths and shrugging off your weaknesses. You have to focus on what you did instead of what you didn't do. When you feel like you can do something better than you did before, even if it won't be easy, *do it*. That is how you breed self-respect. Do the right thing. Stick to your guns. Believe in your purpose. Be a good person.

When someone gives you a compliment, let it sink in and hold it close to your heart. When someone puts you down, let it roll right off you and don't look back. These are practices that are in our power no matter who we are. We can control the way we are affected by our experiences and our relationships. We just have to do it. The more you follow your heart, the more your self-respect will blossom. And from there, believing in yourself is simple. Hold yourself in high esteem. The world is hard enough on us without being equally cruel to ourselves. Recognize any bad habits that might be making you feel bad about yourself and stamp them out.

Another common pitfall worth mentioning while you're still at the beginning of your journey, is the tendency to go *all in*. What I mean by this is similar to trying to do too much at once, but it has a slightly different flavor. A lot of times we fail to achieve what we want because we've been a little too harsh with ourselves. This is best illustrated in dieting terms but it's relevant to anything in life. So for the sake of interest, let's think back to that person I talked about earlier who wanted to lose 100 pounds. And let's say that they've decided to go *all in*. They know, realistically, that they will have to be on this diet for over half a year, but still, they tell themselves that they will not be having any treats during this process at all. No wine, no chocolate, no salty snacks, no sugary drinks, no carbs, no gluten, no sugar, no fun at all. They're just going to have vegetables, protein, and water for over half a year.

Excuse my cynicism, but how awful does that sound? And how long is a resolve like that really going to last? We can't forget what happens when we're all work and no play. Making yourself miserable isn't likely to help you get what you want. It will only lead you to eventually give up, and then beat yourself up for giving up. Life has to be enjoyable! So, even if that person really does need to cut down on their indulgences, they do not have to swear off enjoyment completely in order to lose some weight. Starving themselves of everything they love is only going to make them give up sooner and possibly even gain weight. Keep this in mind when you're setting your goals. That initial burst of motivation at the start of a project is incredible on many levels, but it can be slightly intoxicating; therefore leading you to place unreasonable demands on yourself. Try to keep perspective and remember: all things in time and moderation.

Finally, as you start jotting down your goals and getting your head around what it is you really want to achieve, keep in mind that you will have to reward yourself as you progress. I cannot stress this enough. As partial as I am to the **Tough Love Approach**, you can't have the stick without the carrot. For all the ways human beings are complex, we are equally simple. Generally speaking, we respond well to rewards and we react poorly to punishment. So if you want to get the best out of yourself, schedule some appropriate rewards to mark your progress throughout your journey.

If saving money is your goal, when it's time for a reward, treat yourself by having a movie night in the house with popcorn so that you can enjoy yourself without impeding on your finances. If you start a business and your first year goes well, treat yourself to a weekend away or a new piece of equipment that your business will benefit from. The way in which you reward yourself is as important as the act itself. You don't want to reward yourself with something that's going to set you back. In saying that, I would also stress that if your goal is to lose weight, **try not to reward yourself with food.** The reason behind this theory is that, by rewarding yourself with food you are actually subconsciously telling yourself that the healthy food you've been eating isn't good or isn't enough to satisfy you. Subliminal messages like this can impact the way you feel about the diet you're on and that can, in turn, intercept or halt your progress.

Once again, I do not mean to say that you shouldn't have treats along the way. Moderation is always going to win where weight loss is concerned. But what I mean is that rewarding yourself with a non-food item or activity, will give you the boost you need without derailing your mission. So if it's weight loss you're after, when it's reward time, buy yourself a new top, get your hair done, have a night out with the guys, treat yourself to a new album… whatever is going to make you feel good about what you're doing and motivate to keep on keeping on.

Overall, if you take extra care when planning goals and rewards, you are starting with a dedicated, thoughtful mind. A mind like this will be much more stable in the face of procrastination and any obstacles that may occur along the way. Remember, where you start is just as important as how you finish. Thinking clearly about these things at the beginning of your journey will make holding onto self discipline that much easier.

The Steps Towards Self-Discipline

Before moving onto the next section, here's a quick recap of how to set goals that are going to work *for* you, not against you. Refer to this list anytime you're starting a new project or when you feel like your goals are not as achievable as you thought.

1 - Take baby steps.
Remember that thinking big is good for keeping your dreams alive, but thinking small will help you stay positive and productive for longer. Taking too much on at once could mean running out of steam

before the race even begins. Set smaller goals between yourself and your big goal, and all will move along nicely.

2 - Set realistic goals.
Be good to yourself by setting tasks that you can actually achieve. Achieving goals will boost your self-esteem and give you the extra push you need to keep moving forward in life. Recognize when something might take more time and energy than you have to give right now and leave that for a better time. When setting new goals and assessing current goals, ask yourself if what you're reaching for is attainable. If it isn't, set a few smaller goals leading up to it or re-think that goal altogether. If you set goals that you cannot achieve, you risk taking a hit to your confidence if and when failure strikes.

3 - Keep your plate organized.
If you've got a lot of stuff going on in your life, be realistic about what you can accomplish and how long it'll take to get there. You might need to let go of something in order to make room for the thing you want, or you might need to give yourself some extra time. Remember that putting yourself under too much pressure could fast-track you to failure and all that will do is make things harder on you.

4 - Do what YOU want to do.
Keep your own personal values at the forefront of your mind at all times. There is no point in doing what other people want you to do, if you don't want it for yourself. This is your life and these are your dreams. Even when other people in your life mean well, they mightn't know what's truly right for you. Trust yourself and your instincts. They might be the best resources any of us have.

5 - Believe in yourself!
Even if it feels awkward at the start, believing that you can achieve what you want, is vital fuel for your fire. Give yourself the respect you deserve and keep your chin up. If you have trouble believing in your true potential, you might need to practice a little bit. Start by recognizing every achievement and accomplishment you make, no matter how small. Think of them as building blocks of self-confidence. Let yourself be inspired by them. Let your

accomplishments feed your determination. And let yourself feel good about every single one of them.

6 - Resist the temptation go *all in*.
Putting everything you've got into to something could mean starving yourself of energy and time for anything else in life. Doing this could mean failing at multiple things at once which could be damaging to your self-esteem. Remember to give yourself a break when you need one. You need to treat yourself kindly in order to stay motivated. Don't starve yourself of happiness or turn your life into one big punishment. Efforts like that rarely make it to the finish line. Moderation is the key to success, so pace yourself.

7 - Reward yourself.
Whatever you're reaching for, there is a time to be fierce and a time to be proud. Rewarding yourself gives you a moment to reflect on what you've achieved so far, thus building confidence and motivation that will keep you on the right path. Never underestimate the power of a treat! Giving yourself time to feel good about what you're doing is food for the soul.

"This is a marathon in life. You can't be sprinting all the time or else you wear yourself out. You have to make sure you're taking care of yourself, keeping yourself grounded and not letting every little thing get you worked up."
Brian Moynihan

The Truth About Giving Up – And How To Stop Doing It!

"A dream doesn't become reality through magic; it takes sweat, determination and hard work."
Colin Powell

I doubt that there is anyone in the world who hasn't given up on something they'd once hoped to achieve. Trial and error plays a large and significant role in life. It's how we explore our capabilities. It's how we learn to judge what we can and cannot do; what we're good at and what we struggle with. Each one of us is different from the rest. We are all unique individuals. We all have different talents, interests, and psychological make-ups. We've all had our own personal ups and downs. As children, trial and error helped us develop our identities. It helped shape the view we had of ourselves among our peers, and led us to make many of the decisions that still affect our lives today. At school, we learned what our strengths and weaknesses were, both academically and socially. We found out what tasks we had a flare for and which ones would take more effort to achieve.

Some of us were great students while others were able to use their charm to get them through their early life. Some of us struggled with just about everything we were handed in our youths while others strived when it came to forging a path for themselves. While some of us gave up when faced with harder challenges, others persevered and learned to master the things they struggled with most. One highly contributing factor of these early tendencies was the type of support network we had at home and the way we were raised in general. So too, our teachers and extended families also played a role in our early development.

Some of us will have lost certain abilities as we've travelled through adulthood. An athlete, for example, may have sustained an injury that changed the course of their career. Someone who exhibited great promise as an adolescent may have suffered a tragedy, such as the loss of a sibling or parent, which turned their world upside down. In circumstances such as these, a person would be forced to adapt to the loss of that ability, or to grow stronger after being at their weakest. They might be able to recover quickly and move onto another interest with ease, or they might never quite feel complete again. Such is the nature of individuality and the wildly differing experiences within our species. These are the foundations that we built our adulthoods on. No one has had your life but you. This is why I continually stress the importance of taking a personalized approach to self-improvement.

But no matter who you are, giving up will likely have played a role in your life at one time or another. We all have habits and limits, and these attributes govern our actions and our self-beliefs. Habits form patterns and trends in our behavior. Limits determine the scope of our abilities. There is only so much effort any of us can spend on something before we decide that we've had enough. For some, perseverance comes easily and that makes getting a job done infinitely easier. For others, perseverance mightn't even feature on their radar. There are a lot of people in the world who just can't seem to fight the urge to give up. When the going gets tough, they throw their hands in the air and walk away. If this type of habit is deeply rooted, it might prove incredibly difficult to rewrite; however, doing so is entirely possible.

We have to start by turning our attention inward. Taking time to reflect on the things you've given up on in the past may be difficult or even painful, but exploring your past failures can tell you a lot about your inclination to give up. The more you understand about your past, the more power you will have when it comes to shaping your future. By looking back, we can start to identify our patterns, thus better preparing us for what lies ahead.

Start by asking yourself a few questions.
Are you likely to give up when things get difficult?
Is it possible that the reason you give up is because you're afraid of failure?
Is your self-confidence a bit flimsy and in need of a boost?
Do you suffer from poor self-beliefs or insecurity?

Do you have a short attention span?
Are you likely to self-sabotage? If so, can you identify any feelings beneath that tendency?

There may be any number of underlying thoughts and feelings driving you to give up, so taking the time for *active reflection* will help you understand how you got where you are today. Doing so is truly an invaluable exercise for anyone. Many of us seek the answer to our struggles online or through our friends and family, but the most helpful resources that all of us have, are ourselves and our pasts. The more we know about who we are and why we function the way we do, the more strength and knowledge we can put towards changing the shape of our lives.

Think about how you react when you give up on something.
Are you able to just shrug it off and forget about it?
Does it niggle at you?
Do you beat yourself up about it?
Do you feel ashamed or embarrassed?
Do you feel angry or frustrated?
Do you regret even trying?
Are you itching to give it another try?

All of us will feel differently in these situations but the more we ask ourselves these types of questions, the better equipped we will be when it comes time to knuckle down and try again. When we react with anger or we direct our negative feelings outward, there is usually something deeper going on. Anger is often a mask for more difficult emotions such as sadness, grief, embarrassment, disappointment, fear, and shame. By directing our anger outwards - either at other people or circumstances that are out of our control - we are often avoiding the difficult feelings we're having about ourselves. We are reaching outward because it's easier than looking inward. People with this type of habit often make excuses when they don't see something through to the end. They blame other people, circumstances, timing, the weather, virtually anything as long is it doesn't impede on their conscious self-beliefs. But the problem with habits like these is that they can keep you anchored to the spot. They mask the problem, never giving you the opportunity to improve, change, or make things right. They hold you back from helpful exercises like self-reflection and could gradually lower your self esteem.

This cycle can be so hard to break free from, that we could end up giving up on virtually everything we ever start. If you are the type of person that chronically starts projects but rarely finishes them, is it possible that you are simply so accustomed to giving up - so *used* to it - that you let opportunity pass you by again and again?

The things we want most in life are almost always the hardest things to achieve. So whether you've been dieting on and off for your entire life and still haven't gotten to your perfect weight, or you've wanted to go back to school for years but the timing has never been quite right, the first thing you have to do is accept that the road isn't always going to be easy. There will almost never be a perfect time to start a project. Rarely in life do the stars align and all your troubles disappear to make way for a change. And for this reason, self-discipline can be pretty hard work. Life goes on regardless of what you're reaching for. The world will not stop so that you can smooth out a new path for yourself. The dishes will still need to be done, meals will still need to be cooked, your friends and family will still lean on you in times of struggle, your car may break down, you may lose your job. In the face of life as it stands, getting the things you want can be a long haul. But we have to be able to forge ahead despite that. Everyone deserves the chance to reach higher, and the only person that can give you that chance, is you. You have the power to take life in your stride. You are in control of your own victories and your own shortcomings.

Keep this thought at the forefront of your mind to help you maintain your resolve as you work towards conquering self-discipline. Your past does not have to dictate your future. Failing at something in the past does not mean you are doomed to fail it at for the rest of your life. We have to give ourselves the benefit of the doubt. We are all capable of growth and change. Don't forget that you have to be your own cheerleader in life. You deserve that much!

The Easy Way Out

A lot of times, when things get difficult, we take the easy way out. Maybe that person who wants to lose 100 pounds will give up when they reach twenty pounds. They might try to convince themselves that they're happy with losing a fraction of their original goal but deep down they will probably suffer from feelings of personal disappointment and regret. They allowed themselves to become discouraged. They gave up when the going got tough, and unfortunately doing so will only make things harder on them the next time they try. The habit of giving up gets harder to break with each defeat.

But often, it is *impatience* that really defines when we decide to throw the towel in. We all want instant gratification. We want to go on a diet and see results *today*. We want to be able to maintain that buzz we feel when we initially decide to make a change, but feelings like that are rarely easy to sustain. When you're in something that's going to be a long haul, instant gratification probably isn't going to be a factor, and the sooner you accept that, the better. Even if you stay on track all the way to the end, other aspects and elements of life will still require your attention. That means that the amount of energy and excitability you'll have to put towards your goal will naturally ebb and flow over time. You have to be able to maintain your levels of motivation, to ration them out from beginning to end so that you don't give up before you even get started. And maybe a good way to think about that is to imagine that you only have a certain amount of motivation to put toward any project. If you use up all your motivation during the early stages of a project, it makes sense that you'll lose interest when your motivational systems are depleted. So pace yourself. Reserve some excitement for the middle of your journey when things are likely to be the hardest.

Imagine there was something you could do to earn an extra $1,000 per month. It would be hard work but it'd help you save money, maybe you'd get to buy a new car or go on a special vacation. But after the first month, you run out of motivation. Without that motivation, you become less and less interested in the project. By the third month you're feeling like your systems are depleted. You're tired and grumpy. And just at that moment, you are given the option to take $1,000 outright if you agree to give up now. It's tempting, and a lot of people will choose that option because they simply don't have the motivation to carry on. They're over it. But taking that $1,000 means that that's all you get. You could've had $12,000 at the end of the year but the desire for instant gratification and the inability to maintain your excitement led you astray. If that example feels a little abstract, think about it in dieting terms. Do you give into the desire for instant gratification by eating chocolate every time you crave it, or do you keep the end goal in mind, get some perspective, and stick to your guns?

The thing is, and I cannot stress this enough, finishing tasks is the most important element of self-discipline. The more projects you finish and the more goals you reach, the easier you will find it to conquer the next thing. It's the same theory I mentioned a chapter or so ago about believing in yourself and setting smaller goals that lead up to bigger ones. Setting smaller goals for yourself means that you will *complete* more tasks, and this in turn, will help you prove to yourself that you can do whatever you set your mind to. It will help you build a strong foundation of positive self-belief. It will let you feel more excitement and motivation, more often. If you can't finish projects, or you rarely do, how will you ever be able to summon up the courage to take on the next challenge? How could you be confident that you can stay on track and see something through to the end if you rarely ever reach an ending of anything? How likely are you to succeed? Remember, you will always feel good about reaching goals. The happiness you get from that, the *pride* you feel, is vital for your self-esteem and the ways in which you will approach projects in the future. Think of each achievement you earn as a milestone. Use them to harvest stronger will power.

Did you know that human beings have an innate need for completion? We need finality in our lives. There is something about being able to bring things to an appropriate and successful end that gives us peace. Think about when you're reading a great book or watching a television series that you really enjoy. Do you read one chapter and then set the book aside for weeks at a time? Do you decide to watch one episode of the TV series per month? No. You lose half a night's sleep because you can't wait to find out how the book ends. You binge watch the TV series, and the next four seasons of it, because you have to know what happens to your favorite characters *in the end*. That type of behavior is common because it is rooted in our deep need for completion.

So, with that in mind, think of all the things you've started but haven't finished. Think about that guest bedroom that's still only half painted. Think about the diet you gave up on, the song you started writing but haven't found the time to go back to, the photo album of your children that was supposed to be a week long project but has been sitting in a heap on your coffee table for months. Half finished projects and unrealized goals will undoubtedly weigh on your need for completion. They will quietly eat away at you because you haven't stuck with them long enough to achieve the satisfaction you'd get by finishing them. Now think about things that you have completed and how they've made you feel.

Completing tasks just feels good. It gives us the satisfaction and finality we crave. It allows us to feel a sense of pride, and our completed projects bring joy into our lives. Keep this in mind when you feel the urge to give up. Think of your goal as your favorite TV series. Keep going. Keep pushing. The positivity you will feel when you get there will be well worth the time and energy you put in along the way.

How To End The Procrastination Cycle

"Procrastination is like a credit card: it's a lot of fun until you get the bill."
Christopher Parker

Let's take a minute to think about procrastination. It goes without saying that procrastination is kryptonite to self-discipline. It's the voice that tells us to put something off just a little while longer. It might tell us to give up completely or force us focus on things that are less important than the task at hand. Procrastination is one of the most perplexing psychological tendencies human beings possess. The nature of it is completely nonsensical. It is basically a tool that we use to get in our own way, to halt our own progress. We use it to place a barrier between ourselves and our goals, and there could be endless reasons for doing this. It is possible that our self esteem is suffering or that we're self sabotaging because we're afraid of failure. It might just be a really bad habit that needs to be broken. But whatever its origin, procrastination is unlikely to be a positive force in anyone's life.

The interesting thing about procrastination is that we rarely succumb to it when we're working on things that don't really matter. No one puts off things that are relatively easy. For instance, you could have a hundred things on your to do list; ninety-nine of which are completely inconsequential while only one is extremely important. Procrastination will lead you to accomplish all ninety-nine unimportant tasks before allowing you to even think about the one important task. It's almost like there is something frightening on the horizon; something that might involve difficult emotions, a lot of administration, or the possibility of failure. And in order to avoid these potential negative experiences, we choose to occupy ourselves with virtually any other inconsequential task. I mean, why look at the scary thing on the horizon when you can look at the easy stuff that's right in front of you instead?

One thing that might happen in an instance like this, is that the one *important* thing on the list could begin to seem bigger and bigger the more we avoid it, and this means that we're even less likely to tackle it. Procrastination can very easily make a mountain of a molehill. But unfortunately, it can also do a lot worse than that. It can speak to our subconscious. It tells us that we're not good enough. It tells us that we're failing. It tells us to give up. Procrastination stands in our way and we have to learn how to break through it. We have to be able to stand up to it, face it, and knock it down. This way, we can maintain our feelings of self worth and self-confidence. We can prove to ourselves that we can conquer this and anything else that follows.

Think about how procrastination features in your life. Ask yourself: What is it that you do when you're supposed to be doing something else? And how does not doing it make you feel at the end of the day? If you work from home, are you able to get the job done or are you likely to do the dishes first and maybe clean out a cupboard or two before getting started?

What could you be doing today that you keep pushing back to tomorrow?

How are your stress levels affected by procrastination?

Why do you insist on holding yourself back?

Do you feel like you can rely on yourself?

The next time you get distracted from what you should be doing, prove to yourself that you can accomplish it by saying no to distraction and getting stuck in. When it comes to our self-beliefs, our confidence, and our sense of hope in life, we have to start somewhere, and we have to do it *now*. There is no reason to wait until tomorrow. If you want to quit smoking, I promise you, your lungs will not care whether it's Monday or Thursday. They do not discriminate between morning and night. Whatever it is that you're putting off for another day, start doing it now. Don't let procrastination dictate what you can accomplish and when you cannot accomplish it. You're stronger than that. You are the one in control.

Tendencies to procrastinate are often a method of self-sabotage. Self-destruction and getting in the way of your own happiness is not uncommon and it's a habit that can creep into your life for a variety of reasons. But it's important to be able to recognize if you're being your own worst enemy. It's important to think deeply about this and be honest with yourself. You don't have to tell the whole world or publicly shame yourself over it. But you do need to dig deep and find the root of the problem. Beneath patterns of self-sabotage there are often feelings of fear or worthlessness. These may not be apparent in your conscious mind, and the only way to change them is by being determined to fight the urge to self-sabotage. If you are likely to care for other people before caring for yourself, self-sabotage may feature in your life even more. Focusing your attention on other people, especially when you prioritize other people's happiness above your own, has a way of eating at your ability to care for yourself. It drains your energy and causes you to put yourself last on your list.

Selflessness can be a wonderfully endearing quality but if it is functioning as a means to shift your attention away from yourself, you'll probably need to address it. You have to be able to take care of number one. People who are natural caregivers may find it hard to offer themselves the same love and attention they give to other people, but these tendencies can have detrimental effects on your self esteem and your overall happiness; especially if the people in your life take your kindness for granted or take advantage of you. Remember that caring for yourself and reaching for bigger and better things does not make you selfish. Being able to care for yourself is just as important as caring for other people.

When it comes to self-discipline, it's important to learn to value yourself and your life. When you give up on yourself, you're standing in your own way. You are actively telling yourself that you can't have what you want, and the only person you're hurting is yourself. *You* will be the one who has to live with the consequences. *You* are the one who will feel the disappointment, who will feel like they're stuck in life. You have to accept that you are allowed to dedicate yourself to doing and accomplishing everything you want in your lifetime. You're allowed to live your life to the fullest. Giving up only makes it harder to get back up and try again. It makes your resolve weak and has the power to change how you feel about yourself.

Make no mistake; self-progression takes a lot of courage. Facing the things you want to be better at means believing that you deserve more in life. It is natural to feel a bit unsure of ourselves from time to time. We all struggle with self-doubt. But, as difficult as it may be, taking the time to think more deeply about yourself and your behavior is the best way to create lasting change in your life. In the coming chapters, I will offer you all the practical skills you need to stay focused and manage your time effectively, plus plenty of tips and tricks to keep you on task. But it would be naive to think that we all need exactly the same advice. Think about it, any website can claim to give you five or ten ways to conquer self discipline but do any of us actually believe that *everyone* in the world can succeed with the same formula? Sure, there are plenty of things we can do that most people will benefit from to some extent, but if we want to be able to carry our determination into everything we do in life, it is necessary to get to know ourselves as well as we possibly can. Take your time on this journey. Be kind to yourself and be patient with yourself. Try not to rush. Easy does it.

The only way we can achieve what we want is if we believe we can. So if you have a habit of giving up, it's time to wipe the slate clean and try again. Giving up will have altered your self-beliefs along the way and it's important to start rebuilding. Practice makes perfect. It doesn't matter if you've failed once or a thousand times. Failure doesn't dictate what you can and cannot achieve. Failure merely builds resistance. Use it to encourage you to keep pushing forward. Use it as fuel for your fire. Whatever it is that you want to improve or achieve, tell yourself right now that giving up is not an option. Yes, you will have set backs. Yes, you might not always feel like you're in the best mental state to keep going. Yes, you will face obstacles and you may have to jump a few hurdles. But it's okay to take breaks along the way. It's okay to stop and catch your breath when you need to. Motivation is something we have to *feed* to keep it alive and it's only natural that it will ebb and flow with the tides of our lives. Some days you will wake up feeling ready to take the world by storm. Other days you'll wake up and wish you could stay in bed all day. That's okay, it's normal. Having self-discipline doesn't mean that you have to be in top form all day every day. It just means that you can take life in your stride, get your head back in the game after a fall, and get the job done.

Moving Forward

For your reference, here is a brief recap of this chapter for you to refer to anytime you feel the inclination to give up.

1 - Look inward.

In order to better understand your own personal pitfalls, think deeply about your past experiences. If you recognize that you do have a habit of giving up, think about when and why that pattern started. Try to identify any contributing factors such as low self-esteem or a fear of failure and take some time to explore your deeper feelings. Are you easily bored or do you have a tendency to self-sabotage? Taking a personalized approach means that you will be able to tailor make your progression to self-discipline. Getting to know yourself more deeply means that you will be able to avoid potential pitfalls but it also means that you can identify the root of the problem and eliminate it so as to ensure lasting success.

2 - Don't wait for the perfect time to get started.

Life will not wait for you to get yourself organized. Your schedule will not suddenly become wide open just because you've decided to make a change. All of your responsibilities and your troubles will not magically disappear one day. Waiting for the "right time", is usually just another method of procrastination. If you want to do something, start today. Start *now*.

3 - Be patient.

Instant gratification is a big part of our lives today. Because of the way we communicate with one another nowadays, and the fast pace of life in the twenty-first century, it's easy to become impatient with ourselves and the things we're working on. If something is going to take a while to achieve, you have to let go of your need for instant gratification and *ration your motivation* so that you don't run out of steam at the start of your journey. Pace yourself. And remember, just because you don't see results immediately, does not mean that you're on the wrong path. Trust yourself and try to keep a relaxed state of mind.

4 - Finish as many tasks as possible.

The human need for completion can be a great source of extra motivation and higher feelings of self worth. Every time you finish something, your mood will benefit from it. So, by setting yourself smaller tasks and as many attainable goals as possible, you are setting yourself up for a win. Remember that a large part of being self-disciplined relies on mindset. The human mind is easy to "trick" into feeling good. When you complete tasks, you breed feelings of accomplishment, pride, relief, finality and calmness, as well as boosting your physical and mental energy. So rather than working on many things over a long period of time, consider finishing a task before moving onto the next thing. Finish tasks *before* you become bored of them.

5 - Get your head around procrastination.

Understanding more about procrastination and how it functions in your life is immensely important. Whether you have difficult emotions that need addressing or you simply have a bad habit of putting things off until later, procrastination needs to be addressed and eliminated. If it is allowed to rule your life, procrastination will only leave you feeling frustrated and unsure of yourself. Having something on your to do list for weeks or months at a time is draining, even if you don't realize it on a conscious level. Whatever you've been putting off, do it now. There's no more time to waste.

6 - YOU are in control.

No matter what things have been like up to now, you have the power to build the life you want for yourself. Giving up on yourself is detrimental to your self-esteem. It can make starting new projects extremely difficult and it can make completing tasks virtually impossible. This is your life. You're allowed to focus on yourself. You're allowed to reach for more. You are the one who's in charge. It takes courage to embark on journeys of self-progression, and they're not always easy. But, by dedicating yourself to conquering your bad habits and harnessing self-discipline, you're setting yourself up for a positive future.

"I think a hero is an ordinary individual who finds strength to persevere and endure in spite of overwhelming obstacles."
Christopher Reeve

Practical Thinking For Everyday Success

"Success is not final, failure is not fatal" it's the courage to continue that counts."
Winston Churchill

Before moving onto a deeper exploration of what it takes to really knuckle down and reach your goals, take a little time to familiarize yourself with the following basic rules and everyday skills that will help keep your eye on the prize.

Did you know that if you stick with something for just 21 to 28 days, it's more likely to become a habit? This can be a very helpful thing to keep in mind when you're embarking on something new. Change can be difficult and it can take a while to adjust to. Waking up at 6AM won't be easy for you if you usually get up at 11AM. Becoming a vegan is going to be hard if you eat bacon every day. Though there are people in the world who aren't really phased by change, most of us will find it anywhere from a little bit daunting to completely disorienting.

Whether you are quitting smoking or attempting to change your daily routine completely, it's natural to find new things tricky at the start. But often, by simply knowing that there will come a time in the not too distant future when these things will become dramatically easier, you can keep the perspective you need to carry on. It's only natural to be uncertain about major life changes. Many of us don't even like having to change our plans for Friday night! But, if you make a mark on your calendar for 21 or 28 days from now, that major life change will suddenly seem a lot easier to achieve. You can easily stick with something for a month if you know that it's going to get easier as you progress.

We know by now that thinking too big can mean that we will be more likely to give up, and that by thinking smaller, we will be more likely to stick with our new plans. Focusing on the time it takes to create a new habit means that you will be giving yourself a specific date to look forward to; one that may come a lot sooner than the bigger goal at hand. Having this date in mind means that you will be able to look forward to a time when things are going to get easier; thus, you will be more likely to stick to your guns and carry on doing what you're doing. Self-discipline is like any other positive habit. Give it a few weeks and it will become second nature.

For many people, the most exciting part of major life changes is the planning stage. We go out and buy all kinds of stationery and accordion folders, we make lists and vision boards. But putting our heart and soul into planning could mean that we use up almost all of our time and energy before we even get started. And of course, after that, we run out of steam, especially when the going gets tough and we realize that reaching our goal is going to take longer than we'd hoped. Getting excited about a new project is a great thing, don't get me wrong, but it's important to find a system that's going to work for you and get on with things.

Think about your own behavior and how you're likely to approach new routines.
Do you spend a long time in the planning stages and then give up once you actually get down to the nitty gritty?
Is it possible that, by spending so much time and money buying new equipment and writing lists, you are actually *procrastinating*?
Think about it. Do you have a bunch of kitchen appliances that you've only used a handful of times? A juicer? A blender perhaps? Do you have a cupboard full of half filled diaries or a bunch of unused folders?
What is it they say about the best laid plans? No matter how much you put into the beginning of a project, whether you fail or succeed is more dependent on what happens later.

When you're in the planning stage, it's important to find a system that works for you and get stuck in as soon as possible. Don't wait until you're bored of the idea to finally begin. If you have a friend or family member that is particularly good with organization or time management, ask them what works for them and give it a try. Think about who you are and what has worked for you in the past. If you've tried digital apps before and they didn't work, try something new.

If you tend to write a lot of to do lists but abandon them before you've completed all the tasks, try something new. There's no point in going down a road that you know hasn't worked for you in the past. If you're a great diary user, incorporate your self-discipline progress into your daily entries. Write down what you accomplished, how long it took, what obstacles you faced and how you feel about your progress so far. Write down anything you think you could do better in the coming weeks and months. Write down what you hope to accomplish tomorrow or by the end of the week, and refer to those entries regularly to keep your head in the game.

If you're a particularly busy person who spends a lot of time on-the-go, carrying lists and diaries everywhere you go mightn't be an option for you. Instead, try out a few apps on your mobile phone and see if they might be able to help keep you on task. To-do list apps and other organizational apps can be very helpful. Remember, it's okay to switch your method of organization at any time. If one system isn't working, don't use it as an excuse to give up. Just change up and try something else. If you have a hard time staying focused on one task at a time, try setting a timer and don't let yourself move onto anything else until the alarm goes off. Remember the importance of trial and error. Whatever you do, try not to use your organizational tools as a means for procrastination. Why spend hours planning what you're going to do this week if you have the time and resources to do those things now?

If you really like the idea of making vision boards or writing down lists of goals and positive mantras to keep you on track, it's important to keep it fresh. Becoming bored is very dangerous when you want to achieve self-discipline. If you keep your visual aides in the same place all the time, you'll get so used to seeing them that you'll barely take notice of them after the first week.

So instead of pinning all of your motivational tools on your refrigerator, why not periodically move them to new locations so that you're forced to see them in a new light? Move posters, to do lists, and mantras from the kitchen to the bedroom. Then, from the bedroom to the bathroom mirror. Or, why not write down a new mantra each week to replace the stale ones? The aim is to keep reminding yourself of your goal so that you can keep your momentum up. When you're in something for the long haul, you've got to do everything you can to prevent things from becoming stagnant. This is equally important as your goal itself.

Make things as easy on yourself as possible. For example, if you really want to get in shape, don't sign up for a membership at a gym that's going to cost you a fortune and take an hour to travel to. How are you possibly going to maintain your motivation if your chosen form of exercise is draining your bank account and taking up all your time? Instead, work with what you've got. Maybe there are exercise classes at a different location nearby, or perhaps you could take up running or cycling. Why not recruit a friend to go out walking a few nights per week or go on more adventures with your kids? Sometimes, even when we have all the best intentions, we lead ourselves astray from the start by making things too difficult to achieve and nearly impossible to keep up with.

Remember, your motivation will run out eventually so if you plan for that eventuality, you're less likely to give up when you feel drained or low on energy. Don't give yourself tasks that you're likely to give up on because they don't fit into your life as it is today.

The same goes for virtually every aspect of self-discipline. If you're going to start working from home, get rid of any possibility for distraction. Do your housework on the evenings and weekends so as to resist the temptation to get up and clean when you should be working. Set a timer for the amount of time you should be working and don't let yourself get up until it goes off. If you work on a laptop, consider going out and working at a different location like a coffee shop or the library to keep yourself from stagnating. If you're likely to be distracted by Facebook or other websites when you should be working, purchase an app that will block those websites during certain hours of the day. If you want to change your eating habits, clear out your refrigerator and don't keep treats in the house anymore. If you want to drink less, remove alcohol from the house and change the way you socialize with your friends.

The bottom line is, the easier you make things on yourself, the more likely you are to succeed. So, take the time to declutter. Declutter your office and your fridge, and most importantly, declutter your mind. Strip things down to basics. Decluttering your mind may be a concept that seems a bit abstract at first. But each one of us has an inner voice and many times it is this voice that's holding us back.

When we're trying to concentrate, our inner voice distracts us by reminding us of the *other* things we should or could be doing. It thinks obsessively about the conflicts we may be dealing with at any given moment. It dwells on negative emotions such as loss, rejection, and shame. It may throw overly critical comments at us when we're doing our best to get ahead. It tells us that we're not good enough. Many times when we're trying to stay focused, our thoughts lead us astray. This might be because we're under a lot of pressure or because we're struggling with self-doubt or poor self-beliefs. But whatever it is that you can't seem to get out of your mind, be honest with yourself about it, and do everything you can to silence that inner chatter.

If you can't focus on the task at hand because there are things you need to accomplish and you can't stop thinking about them, do everything you can to get them done so that you can get down to business as soon as possible. If there are items on your to do list that are likely to hang around for a while, do what you can with those things *now* and then let yourself to forget about the rest until you can attend to them. Tell yourself that you've done everything you can at this stage, and let it go.

You know that one of the basic principles of self-discipline is being committed to giving yourself credit where credit is due. If it's self-doubt that you're combating, this is particularly important. You might have to fight for your life to get that doubt to ease up. Building up positive self-beliefs takes time and practice, but one of the best ways you can beat it, is by giving yourself praise every time you achieve something. Even if you just stayed on task for an hour or two, give yourself credit. The reason I stress this so much is because positive reinforcement is extremely powerful when it comes to bettering yourself and your life.

Think about the things you've accomplished in the past and use those as beacons of hope for your future. Think about the things you haven't accomplished in the past and burn them up to make fuel for your fire. Be on your own side. Be empathetic with yourself when you make mistakes. Forgive yourself. And when it's time to pick yourself up and go again, do so with gusto. Recognize when you put yourself down or when you're unnecessarily harsh with yourself and let go of that behavior. Being cruel to yourself will not serve you. It will only distract you from reaching your goals. Finally, if there are deeper issues holding you back, consider addressing them by talking to a professional or confiding in a friend that you trust. Life is too short to waste time on self-loathing and feelings of defeat. The sooner you get those things out of your way, the better.

If your life is highly demanding and you're juggling a lot of things at once, try to pare down the amount of decisions you have to make each day. Making decisions takes a lot of brainpower and if your schedule is swamped, being forced to make decisions on top of having a heap of responsibility in your life, could cause an increase to your stress levels and a decrease to your productivity. Remember that decisions aren't just the big things we worry about day in and day out. They come in many shapes and sizes. Decisions cover everything from what you're going to wear to work, to what school you're going to send your children to. Everything from what you eat for lunch, to whether or not you're going to make an offer on a new house.

So think about some ways that can you can make things easier on yourself where decisions are concerned. How can you make decisions less taxing on you from day to day? You can start by planning ahead. Why not take some time on a Sunday evening to plan your meals for the week? That way, when it comes time to packing the kids' lunches in the morning or making dinner after a long day at work, the decision will have already been made. Remember to plan your meals based on how much time you're likely to have each day. If you know you're going to be coming home late one night, don't plan on cooking a meal that's going to take hours to prepare. You could also plan what you're going to wear each day of the week so that your mornings are less stressful. This is also a great way to manage your time if you tend to run late in the mornings.

By being able to simply refer to a sheet of paper that tells you what to wear, what to eat for breakfast, and what to feed the kids, you are reserving your brain power for harder and more important decisions that may arise as the day progresses. If you have a family at home, plan out how the week will be organized ahead of time. Who is going to get the kids to and from school each day? Who will be in charge of the grocery shopping this week? Who is going to take the car to get fixed and when? Who's in charge of making appointments to see the dentist? Taking the time to do these things in advance means smoother interactions within the family and less stress all around.

Another great way to reduce the amount of decisions you make each day is by delegating responsibility and tasks to other people. For instance, why not let your spouse choose and prepare a few meals each week? Why not ask a sibling to take charge of a few family matters instead of insisting on doing everything yourself? If you have some less important decisions to make in work, perhaps you could have a coworker take charge of them so you can focus on more important things. The aim here is to do everything you can to make self-discipline as easy on yourself as possible. Reduce the amount of difficulty and confusion in your life, and increase the amount of preparedness and organization; because nothing derails self-discipline like a difficult life. The more we can simplify our lives, the easier it will be reach our goals.

One of the best tricks to ensure success is to tell people what you're working towards. Whatever it is that you're reaching for, if you tell a friend or loved one about it, you're more likely to stick with it. This works for a few reasons. For one, your loved ones will want you to succeed. So in a way, you're creating a support system for yourself by letting other people in. Secondly, if you're stubborn or set in your ways, telling people about your goal could mean that you're more likely to succeed. Stubbornness is often thought of as a negative quality but it can also work to your advantage. If you tell someone that you are going to succeed, being stubborn could provide you with the determination to stick with it no matter what. Many people who consider themselves to be stubborn, don't like to fail. So, it's possible that your stubbornness might just keep you on track if you give it a supporting role in your journey. By telling as many people as you can, you can ensure that your resolve will be even stronger. Eventually, people will ask you how things are coming along and you'll feel a lot better if you get to answer positively than if you have to tell people that you've given up.

Think about how you're likely to behave when you *have* to do something versus when you just *want* to do something. For example, why might someone be more likely to accomplish a task if it is set for them by their employer than they would be if they were self employed? If the task at hand is about personal integrity or financial advancement, surely the goal is equally important whether you're your own boss or not. Right? Wrong. These things are not always that simple. If you're your own worst enemy, being self-employed and staying on task could be excruciatingly difficult. At least when you have a boss telling you what to do, the consequence of not completing a task is daunting enough to see you through. When you're the one in charge, it's easy to let yourself get away with half finished projects. So, if you know that you work better when someone else places a deadline on you, do that for yourself by telling other people about your plans. Recruit a friend to send you an encouraging text each day or tell your family that you might need some extra encouragement for a while. If you work better when someone else is in charge, give yourself someone to answer to. It's that simple.

One thing to keep in mind is that you should be careful about who you tell when you're moving toward a life change. If there are people in your life who are regularly unsupportive or disbelieving of your resolve, you might be better off keeping them out of the loop on this one. Telling someone whom you know is likely to be cynical, sarcastic, or downright rude, is really just a form of self-sabotage. Remember that in life, we need to build relationships with those who lift us up, rather than clinging to the people who put us down. This doesn't mean you have to end your less-than-desirable relationships, but it might be wise to limit what you tell to whom.

Another way to keep yourself on the right path is to plot your progress. Think of this like a map of America and imagine that you are traveling in the hopes of visiting every major city. For each city you explore, you get to put a red pin in the map. As your red pins increase, you'll really be able to gauge just how far you've travelled. You'll be able to physically see how much further you have to go to reach your goal. By plotting the progress of your chosen journey, you'll be marking every accomplishment you make along the way, thus giving yourself increasing positive reinforcement and motivational fuel. If you're writing a memoir, for instance, make a note of each major life experience you write about and as time goes by, let yourself feel good every single time that list grows.

If you're hoping to run a marathon, take note of each time you run further or faster. Let your progress motivate you to keep pushing onward. If you're studying for a degree, mark each milestone along the way with a diary entry. For each step you take on your journey, give yourself a reward to keep up your momentum. Rewards keep the creative juices flowing and make it easier to envision yourself reaching your goals. When things don't go your way, don't let that discount how far you've come. Brush it off, forgive yourself, and move on.

The Practical Level

As I mentioned briefly earlier, it's important to give yourself breaks. Thinking in black and white terms or having an "all or nothing" attitude can lead you to give up anytime you slip up. It can cause you to overwork yourself and then beat yourself up for feeling exhausted. We have to remember that most of our journeys will take a few steps forward and a few steps back regardless of how much we want something or how hard we work for it. We all need a break sometimes. We need to be able to relax and breathe. We need to be gentle with ourselves.

On a practical level, there are plenty of ways to gain and maintain a work / rest balance in life. If you tend to go at things full steam ahead, you would probably benefit from scheduling in your breaks the same way you would schedule in the things you *have* to do. Within each day, schedule in breaks for lunch, a walk, or fresh air. Each week, schedule in at *least* one or two things that you will do for pleasure alone. Take a bath and bring a book in with you. Go out for a run. Go shopping or meet a friend for a drink. Visit the beach for a day. Attend a meditation or yoga class. Whatever will help you to relax. Doing this is vital for your physical and mental health. It is a way to avoid becoming bored with your routine, relieve stress, and recharge your batteries. Do not underestimate the importance of enjoyment in life.

Human life is complicated. I don't know if there is anyone on earth who only has one thing going on at any given time. Whatever we are hoping to achieve will be limited or impacted in some way by the other things we have going on simultaneously. If you work from home and your child is home sick, you might not be able to focus enough to reach your daily target. If you've suffered a bereavement, you might need to take some time to feel and cry before you can regroup and get back on schedule. Think about the possibility of setbacks when you're in the planning stage of a project and schedule in some time for the unexpected so that you're not thrown too far off course if and when they strike. Another way you can combat setbacks is by getting ahead whenever you can. If you've got some extra time on your hands one week, work a little bit harder so that you're ahead of the game. This way, if something goes wrong in another part of your life, you'll still be more or less on track when the dust settles.

We have to be able to realistically assess our lives and treat ourselves accordingly. If you're likely to be unreasonably hard on yourself or you rarely give yourself time to relax, you will probably need to address that. Putting too much pressure on yourself might lead you into cycles of stress, failure, and negative self-beliefs. Remember, taking time out is not giving up. If you make a mistake or you're having a hard time juggling your self-discipline with other things in your life, try treating yourself like a friend.

What would you say to someone else in the same position? Would you criticize them for being unfocused when other things in their life require their energy or would you be understanding and kind to them? Would you put someone down if they were under a lot of stress and their work suffered for it or would you offer them compassion and encouragement? We have to be able to offer ourselves the same kindness and appreciation that we give to others. Giving yourself time to feel good and relax, is just as important as working hard. We rarely work at our best capacity when we're exhausted and weary.

Finally, be sure to focus plenty of your energy on your physical and mental wellbeing. None of us will be able to achieve all we want if we don't look after ourselves properly. We all need to eat well, sleep well, and get plenty of exercise. If you're overtired, you're more likely to become distracted and give up more easily. You won't have the energy you need to conquer each day. If you're hungry all the time, your moods will be less stable and your patience will be compromised. Being well rested and keeping your blood sugar even means that you will be able to think more clearly and make better decisions. If you don't get enough exercise, your physical well being will suffer, your energy will be lower, and you will have less opportunity to secure sufficient endorphins to keep your mood elevated.

Most importantly, human beings have a fundamental need for *play*. Recreation is a vital part of our existence and our overall happiness in life. We all need to be around likeminded people. We all need to blow off steam. Reserving a decent amount of energy for your own personal enjoyment is a fantastic way to de-stress and boost your motivation. There are so many of us that neglect this aspect of life. We sacrifice our enjoyment for work, time and time again. We spend more time doing the things we have to do and less time doing the things we want to do. Maybe you rarely get out with your kids on the weekends because of all the things that need doing around the house. Maybe you give up your hobby because of high demands at work. Maybe you don't see your friends very often because you're always too busy to make time for them. If you're likely to give up the time you spend on pure enjoyment, your mood is likely to suffer and you will be less likely to achieve what you're working toward.

Our psyches need to be fed. We need to be around people who stimulate our minds. We need to do some things that are just for fun. This is an extremely important thing to keep in mind in this day and age. As a society, our fundamental need for play is often overshadowed by the desire for success and our need to classify one another within a financial hierarchy. Who we are within our social groups has taken precedent over how much we actually enjoy our lives. I do not mean to imply that it is bad to give into these pressures per se. I only mean to reiterate the importance of lightness and laughter in our lives. Staying true to yourself and being good to yourself should be a top priority. So be sure to schedule in some playtime each week. Schedule in some physical activity and some relaxation. Eat and sleep at regular intervals. Be good to your mind, body, and soul.

Ten Steps To Keep Motivation High

Before moving onto the next section, here's a quick recap of the practical skills covered in this chapter. Refer to this list anytime you feel your motivation draining or when your routine leaves you feeling stagnant or underwhelmed.

1 - Make a mark on your calendar for 21 days from now.
Knowing that things will become easier after you've had a change in place for three to four weeks, means that your resolve will stay stronger for longer, and your first goal will be realized much sooner. It is easier on the mind to think in smaller time spans. If you hang in there for 21 to 28 days, your new routine will become habit, making the rest of your goal much easier to attain.

2 - Find a system that works and get stuck in.
Don't spend all your time buying new things or planning obsessively. Try out a few different ways to keep yourself motivated and keep moving forward. Ask your best organized friends for some

tips on organization and prioritizing tasks. Use a paper diary if you're used to journaling. If you're not used to carrying a diary around with you everywhere you go, don't waste your money on one. Instead, get an app on your phone that will keep your to do list in order. Try setting a timer for how long you need to stay on task and don't let yourself take a break until the alarm goes off. Remember that trial and error is a good thing. If you try something and it doesn't seem to be working, toss it aside and move onto another method. If you find something that works, stick with it. Just be careful not to waste too much time and energy on this stuff. The important thing is getting the job done.

3 - Keep it fresh.
Don't let yourself become bored by old vision boards or abandoned to do lists. Place your goal lists in new places every week or so, so that they can continue to spur you on as you progress. Try new mantras and write new lists when you tire of the old ones. Add in new organizational methods when things start to become stagnant. The key is to keep reminding yourself of why you started working on something in the first place.

4 - Make things easy on yourself.
Get rid of distraction and eliminate temptation. Declutter your home, office, and mind. Be on your own side and rid yourself of negative thought patterns. Silence any negative inner voices that are hurting you. Don't create schedules that will be impossible to keep up with. Do everything you can to make sure you'll stick with it. Avoid making plans that you're likely to cancel. Instead of letting tasks build up and cause added stress, do anything you can do now. If you find yourself fretting, remind yourself that you've done all you can for the time being.

5 - Reduce daily decision making.
By planning ahead for day-to-day things such as what you will eat and wear each week, you will be reserving your brainpower for more important decisions. Take some time to make plans at the start of the week so that you and the whole family will have an easier time of things. When everyone knows what's going to happen in advance, the likelihood of confusion and unwanted quarrels will be greatly

reduced. Also, by delegating tasks to other people at home or at work, you are giving yourself more brain energy to work with and therefore, more possibility for success.

6 - Tell people what you're up to.
Having a good support system is vital when it comes to making changes and keeping your head in the game. Having a "boss" might be beneficial if you have a hard time staying on task. Plus, by telling people your goals, you're more likely to keep going out of stubbornness alone! Ask someone you trust to give you a little confidence boost when you need one. Just remember to limit what you tell people that are likely to be unsupportive or overly critical of you. Protect yourself from negativity wherever possible by surrounding yourself with people who are positive and hopeful.

7 - Plot your progress.
Stopping to take note of your advancements is food for the soul. It helps you see how much you can achieve when you put your mind to it and also provides you with a moment to relax and reward yourself. It always helps to be reminded of how far you've come. Keeping track of your progress will help you celebrate your accomplishments as they mount up. Plus doing so will motivate you to continue on your path.

8 - Get ahead when you can.
Planning for the unexpected by doing extra work when you've got some spare time, means that you're less likely to be thrown off course when life rears its ugly head and throws you something that you're not prepared for. In the planning stages, you might want to give yourself an extra week or two when penciling in deadlines to avoid having to push them back when things don't go as planned. Being behind on deadlines can be very stressful. So, by extending them from the start, you're not only leaving room for real life, but you're also more likely to get things done on time or ahead of time.

9 - Give yourself breaks.
Sacrificing your enjoyment of life isn't necessary and it will only lead you to feel tired, stressed out, or resentful. We all need to take time to relax and feel good about our accomplishments. We all need

to strike a work / play balance. Relaxation helps the mind recover and prepares you for the next round. If we don't give our minds a chance to rest, the quality of our work will suffer. If we go at life with too much fury, we may forget to actually enjoy ourselves in the process. Remember, if times are hard, don't beat yourself up. Just let yourself take some time to process and regroup. Then, get back at it when things ease up a bit.

10 - Be good to your body and mind.
Make sure that you take care for your physical self as it plays a major roll in productivity and overall happiness. Get plenty of exercise. Be sure to eat healthy foods at regular intervals to keep your mind focused and your moods stable. Try to go to sleep at the same time each night and wake up at the same time each day. Having a physical routine is great for keeping the mind at its most powerful. Plus, sleep gives your body time to process the day. We dream in order to make sense of the things that are happening our waking lives. Our bodies need to be cared for, regardless of what we're working towards. Most importantly, do not underestimate your need for personal enjoyment and fun. In the grand scheme of things, play is just as important as work. We all need to blow off steam sometimes. We need to feel light. We need to smile and laugh.

"Optimism is the faith that leads to achievement."
Helen Keller

How To Get What You Want

"A dream becomes a goal when action is taken toward its achievement."
Bo Bennett

You already know that getting what you want out of life isn't going to happen by simply following a generic set of rules. There are, of course, certain foundation elements of self progression that we could all use to become more disciplined with ourselves; however, we are likely get a lot more out of ourselves if we take a more personal approach. You and your life are unique, and your self-progression will naturally reflect that. The type of person you are, what your upbringing was like, how you respond to certain social situations, your likes and dislikes… all of these things are as unique as your DNA.

For this reason, throughout this book, I have encouraged you to embark on some *active reflection* about yourself as a person. I've suggested that you take time to think deeply about any inclinations you might have in regard to giving up, and how giving into those inclinations makes you feel. What was it that got in your way in the past? Have you let go of your dreams the older you've gotten? Have you held yourself back in life? Are you subject to bouts of self-sabotage? Can you identify any patterns or trends in the way you think, feel, or behave?

Self-reflection and personal analysis are great tools for helping us identify our negative patterns and recognize our potential saboteurs. At this stage in your journey, it may be beneficial to strip things back to basics and start again. I'd like to encourage you to take some time now to think about how settling for less in life has or could affect you. Each time we give up on ourselves, we are subconsciously telling ourselves that we are not good enough. We are telling ourselves that we deserve less. That we're not worth the fight. We are allowing our positive self-beliefs to be chipped away at and reformed. And not only does settling for less affect how we feel about ourselves, it may also affect how we think and feel about other people, and how they in turn, think and feel about us. Our loved ones may become frustrated with us. Our friends may stop believing in us. The people that offer us the most support might begin to feel drained or helpless when we seek their guidance.

The longer discontentment is allowed govern your life, the more altered your relationships and your view of yourself will become. Living a life without self-discipline, or one with many failures accumulating at one time, can force the scales of self-belief to tip the wrong way. The fact is, life can be really hard. And the older we get, the more jaded we may become. The more failures and hardships we are forced to face, the more we lose our youthful outlook on life. But we have to learn how to tap back into that well of excitement. We have to be able to start believing in ourselves again, no matter what brought us to where we are now. We have to feel hopeful no matter how difficult things have been nor how long they've been that way. We have to let go of our pasts and look forward to our futures.

Self-discipline is about both thoughts and actions. Our bodies can only achieve so much when our head's not in the game. But no matter how lost we may be at times, no matter how defeated or depleted we may feel, we *can* reclaim our youthful vitality. By looking back over our past and actively recognizing the times we overcame difficult situations, we can breed new hope and stronger resolves. We need to be able to look back over our lives and hone in on the positive stuff. Achievements are, in themselves, great tools for motivation. The ability to recognize every small feat in life is a virtue. It can give us that extra push we need to keep moving forward, to tell ourselves that we can do this, to remind ourselves that our hard work is paying off. This means finding the positive amidst the negative, locating the optimism beneath the pessimism. It means silencing your inner bully and amplifying your inner cheerleader.

It is important to think back to times when things were difficult but we stayed afloat. Times when we survived. *Achievements* don't have to be big things. They don't have to be things that you earned trophies for. They aren't just the things you've celebrated. *Achievements* are every single time you hung in there when it felt like the whole world was against you. It is an *achievement* to fight the urge to stay in bed all day and actually get up and get things done. It is an *achievement* to get back up when life knocks you down. A lot of times, we put ourselves down for how affected we get by the difficult times in life. We say, "I'm flailing", "I'm struggling", "I'm not handling this well", when in fact, the truth is, you *are* handling it. You're still here. You're still going. You're still fighting. You may have lost many battles, but you're winning the war. It doesn't help to put yourself down when times are hard. These are the moments you need to be able to give yourself credit.

What we really need is the ability to recognize our saboteurs and stamp them out. And that starts within. We need to be able to see the good in ourselves, to feel our own strength and keep our heads held high no matter what. We need to recognize our harmful patterns and rewrite them. We need to be able to learn from our failures, and then get up and try again. Because all of these things are *achievements*. All of them can help to light the fire under you that you need to become self-disciplined. We never have to settle for less just because we've gotten less in the past. It is never too late to change and grow.

The thing about self-discipline is that it really must come from the *self.* As the author of this book, I cannot jump out of the text and force you to get to work. You have to be able to do that for yourself. So, when you want to accomplish something, start by not giving yourself the option to do something else instead. If you've already planned what you're going to have for dinner every day this week, don't allow yourself to veer from those plans. If you've decided that you need to sit down and do some work, don't get up and reorganize your closet. This is something that *you* have to be able to do for yourself. You have to stop talking about what you want to do and start doing it. With practice, motivating yourself to get to work will naturally become easier. Each time you resist distraction, make a note of it. Feel good about it. Give yourself credit. Because every single moment you stay on task is an *achievement*. Every day you stay on track should be used as a tool to prove to yourself that you can get what you want out of life. But you do have to start somewhere, and that much is up to you.

It is important that you focus on *today*, every day. Especially if you are reaching for something that's going to take a long time to achieve. Goals that span far into the future can be too abstract to really get a handle on. This means that they will naturally be easier to give up on. If there are no immediate consequences of giving up, and very few immediate rewards to reap, it makes sense that most of us won't see any long-term goal though to the end.

Think about it. What is the *immediate* consequence when a self-employed person decides to take a day off versus the *future* consequence of the same action? The immediate consequence could be something quite insignificant such as not meeting their daily quota. But they're the one who sets their quota anyway, so it's not like they have a boss to reprimand them for it. Therefore, the immediate consequence is barely felt at all. But the future, or *cumulative consequence*, could prove to be much greater. If it's easy to take one day off, a self-employed person might then decide to take a few more days off, or maybe a week. Eventually, the cumulative consequence is going to set in, and it will likely come in the form of reduced wages and a heap of work that is impossible to get through in the limited amount of time they've left themself with.

Think about the person who's trying to lose 100 pounds. What is the immediate consequence of that person eating a piece of cake? Is anything bad likely to happen while they're eating the cake? No. But the future consequence is pretty serious. What could happen is a domino effect of consequences. This person's weekly weigh-in might not go too well and that might lead them to give in and eat another piece of cake. Because, why not? That week was just a wash out, right? But one week can turn into two. And two pieces of cake can snowball into a whole cake. And a whole cake might mean tossing the whole dieting thing out the window and giving up completely. But, if we focus on doing everything we can do *today*, we are keeping ourselves in the game. If we do everything we can to prevent future consequences, we're likely to stay on the right path. We are moving in the right direction.

There will be many times in all of our lives that we will be tempted to put something off until tomorrow. But how often do you actually come back and do that thing? If you give yourself permission to push something into tomorrow, what's to say that you won't then push it into the next day and then the next? You have to start somewhere and there is no better time than now. Putting things off until later is a very easy way to start a cycle of procrastination. If you want something bad enough, do it now. Do it while you're thinking of it. Do it while it's fresh in your mind. The fact is, the things we put off until Monday, rarely get done. The things that we believe can wait until tomorrow have little or no immediate consequences so we really have to force ourselves to get them done. If the changes you want to make are truly important to you, there's no time to waste. Do it now. Get the ball rolling now.

Keeping perspective on time is one of the most important aspects of self-discipline. Often the things we're reaching for will take longer than a single day to achieve, so we have to be able to think clearly about how long a month or a year really is. What's in a day? If it's going to take you half a year to lose a hundred pounds, is that actually a long time? In the context of your whole life, is six months really too much to give when it comes to good health and vitality for yourself? If you need to save money, is it really a huge sacrifice to save for five years when you might live to be ninety-five? If you've decided to stop drinking for a month to detox and get more done, does it have to be such a big deal? One month is hardly a long time in the context of your life.

Thinking about time in this way can stop you from blowing things out of proportion. The ability to gain and maintain perspective helps in so many aspects of life. Think about your desire for self-progression. You want to learn how to be self disciplined and you know that creating new, healthier habits may take you around twenty-eight days. But don't you deserve that much? You can easily put in twenty-eight days. If you truly value yourself and the direction your life is headed, twenty-eight days is nothing. After those few weeks, you know you'll feel stronger. You'll be able to put in even more. If you're really determined, you will keep prioritizing your self-progression for the rest of your life. But it's worth it, isn't it? To truly believe in yourself, to be able to rely on yourself, to feel hopeful about the future, to secure deep rooted self confidence so that you can live the life you want… surely, designating a portion of your time and energy toward self progression is worth it. Perspective is all about gaining mastery over your own mind and practicing that skill until it becomes second nature. It's about breaking down the walls of apprehension and allowing yourself to get what you really want out of life.

This thought leads me to one of the biggest pitfalls of personal progression: making excuses. I touched upon this topic briefly earlier but it certainly bears repeating and exploring more deeply. There are a good many of us that consistently grab onto anything we can use to lead ourselves astray. We get in our own way and then we blame every force that's out of our control, rather than being honest with ourselves, fessing up and facing the music.

It can be hard to recognize when your excuses are actually valid versus when you're actually just self-sabotaging. However, if you explore your tendencies with an honest and curious mind, you might be able to spot and reverse your harmful patterns. Just be careful not to use exercises like this to beat yourself up. This way of thinking should be productive, not destructive. The aim is to recognize what's going wrong and turn it around. In the interest of productivity, the "why's" in this case are far less important than the "how's". If you want to get to the root of the problem so that you can fix it and move on with your life, forget about *why* you've held yourself back for the time being and instead, focus on *how* you can be better to yourself.

You should know by now that people who are prone to making excuses will almost always wait for the "right time" before making a change. They will rely on conditions being perfect before getting started and then, they will rely on conditions *remaining* perfect in order to stick with their plans. Imagine that you'd like to take a walk every evening, but one night it's raining so you take the night off. The next night you're just too tired to face it. The night after that you're just feeling a bit "blah". In another few days, your resolve is gone completely. Your new running shoes begin to gather dust in a corner. Later, you'll sell them on eBay; relics of lost intentions.

Making excuses is a very easy habit to get into, and the only way you will ever be able to break that habit is by being honest with yourself. You will never be able to get what you want until you own up to your own behavior. Imagine that you have a tendency to give up on relationships when things get hard. You blame the other person or any other circumstance you can think of when deep down, you're actually just scared of commitment. But the thing is, being afraid of commitment is natural and it's really quite common. And if you actually just owned up to that fear and explored your feelings a little more deeply, you might've found the answer to your fear. Next time, you'd have been able to recognize your negative pattern and intercept it before things went wrong again.

Similar to many difficult emotions, excuses are often a mask for something deeper; something more difficult to face. And for this reason, most of us will deny the fact that we're making excuses when we are. Very often, beneath our excuses lie deep-rooted insecurities. These are things that will get in your way time and time again if you don't give them the recognition they need in order to be resolved. There are people who live in such painfully repetitive cycles of attempted change and defeat that their lives never really change, no matter how hard they try. They seek happiness in external things. They want things to change but they can't seem to put the work in. They can't seem to stick with it. They blame the weather. They blame their low income. They blame time. But the blame game doesn't get them anywhere and chances are it's all really just a smoke screen for what lies beneath.

Often, what holds us back is low self-esteem, poor self-beliefs, or periodic bouts of depression. These struggles may come and go throughout our lives and they can affect anyone, regardless of their background or social standing. Often, these emotional parasites rear their ugly heads after a difficult time, like enduring a break-up, the loss of a job, or a bereavement. Of course, there are some people who are simply predisposed to periods of low mood. Some are affected by the dark days of winter while others experience dark moments even on the sunniest days; both literally and metaphorically speaking. Low self-esteem can be caused by any number of negative life experiences from being neglected in childhood to being out-shined by a co-worker or friend in adulthood.

And the thing is, if deep down, we don't believe that we're worth the effort, we're unlikely to give it to ourselves. We will get in our own way again and again. We will make excuses and end up back at square one over and over. We have to be able to value our existence enough to give ourselves a chance for change. If you have bought this book, you recognize that something has to change if you ever want to reach your goals. You recognize that you struggle with self-discipline. It takes a lot of courage to own up to that, and you should be proud of yourself for getting to that point. But now you have to think more deeply about your patterns. Is it possible that the biggest thing holding you back is yourself? If so, isn't it time to change that? Isn't it time to be good to yourself? To allow yourself a chance for success and happiness? To let the past fall away from you and walk hopefully into the future?

There is only one constant that any of us can rely on in life. There is only one thing that we will always have, and that is *ourselves*. We have to offer ourselves enough appreciation and love to be good to ourselves; to treat ourselves with patience, respect, and kindness. We have to allow ourselves the possibility of achieving our goals. The next time you hear yourself making excuses, or getting in your own way, think again. Think deeper. Have the courage to look inward. Fix the faulty wiring and try again. If you do these things and you do them often, the results will be astounding.

Before you embark on a new project, think about any potential consequences and rewards that my lie ahead. The gift of foresight can be a powerful tool to help you avoid mistakes and keep yourself pushing onwards. By keeping the final reward in mind, you might be able to shake the need for instant gratification when it arises. I have encouraged you to steer clear of thinking big, but if you feel yourself starting to give up, it might help to think back to the reason you started in the first place. Thinking about your original goal or talking about it with a friend could help re-spark your interest and get you feeling inspired again. Think about any resources you might have that could light a fire under you. Perhaps you have a family member who achieved what you're trying to achieve. Talking to them about their journey could provide you with the comfort and encouragement you need when times are hard. Seeing their success could make you feel more excited about achieving your own.

Tapping into your resources is not to be underestimated. When it comes to knowledge or people that might be able to assist you, the more the merrier. Being able to ask for and accept help is a virtue. Also, if you can learn from your past mistakes and your past triumphs, do so. Think about how and why you reached some of your goals in the past and use it to your advantage this time. How did you motivate yourself to keep going in the past? What techniques have you used in the past that might be of assistance now? Is there anyone you know that might be able to help you when you hit an obstacle? Is there anyone who has knowledge that you need? You don't have to do everything alone in order to feel good about it. Sometimes it takes more courage to ask for help than it does to plough through life like a lone soldier.

Furthermore, if you know that you might be led astray by something in the future, keeping that in mind will be of great benefit to you. For instance, if you tend to give up on weight loss when you have a disappointing weigh-in on the scales, do yourself and favor and don't weigh yourself too often. If you tend to give up when your workload is particularly heavy, chip away at it every day rather than letting it build up. If you hate rainy days, get some indoor exercise plans in place. These may seem like obvious ideas but, accepting your own bad habits and doing what you can to interrupt them is an easy way to keep you on the right path. Our habits are great resources when it comes to getting to know ourselves better and making changes for the future. When we're honest with ourselves about our own limitations, we're avoiding the disillusionment of failure. We are creating the best possible climate for change.

When time are tough, think about what you're *giving* yourself rather than what you're keeping from yourself. If it's weight loss you're working towards, don't think about the foods you *can't* have. Think about what *can* have: good health, more energy, and a longer life to name a few. If you're saving money, don't place your focus on the things you're not allowing yourself: new clothes, an extra vacation, or a new car. Instead, focus on what you're giving yourself in the long run: a new house, better financial stability, or an education for your children.

Remember as well, that the more you prove to yourself that you can see things through to the end, the healthier your self beliefs will be, and the greater self discipline you will have to carry into the future. Mindset has a lot to do with what we actually accomplish in life. So as you progress on your journey, take plenty of time to ask yourself: *Why* do I want to achieve this goal? Because it is *that*, that needs to be at the forefront of your mind when you're tempted to give up, not doubt or worry. Not how hard you'll have to work to get there. If you want something bad enough, you have to keep your eye on the prize. You have to be dedicated to reaching the final goal.

Remember that when you hit a bump in the road - whether you make a mistake or just you lose your way for a while - all is not lost. We all have days, weeks, and months when things don't go our way. None of us are perfect. Life happens. We will make the wrong choices sometimes, we'll do or say things that don't represent our best selves. But, and I cannot stress this enough, there is no going back to square one in self-progression. Setbacks will occur in life, difficult situations will strike, but the work you put towards getting the life you want is never lost. It never goes backwards. It never goes away. Self-progression only moves forward. It can only snowball into something bigger and better. Think of self-progression as a star on your psyche. In your lifetime, every night you look up at the sky, you will see the same stars. But they are also there in the daytime.

Even when you can't see them, they're there. Every step you take towards making a better life for yourself is like another star that you've earned. It's a little speck of light that will be there for as long as you live. Even when you can't see them, they're there. So, try not to let yourself be discouraged when things get difficult or when it seems like your progression is slowing to a halt. Don't beat yourself up over it. We will all have blips and pauses, no matter what we're trying to achieve. But "square one" does not exist, so don't let yourself fall into the trap of believing you've undone all your hard work just because you're stuck in a rut.

No matter who you are or what it is you want to achieve, you will inevitably face moments of uncertainty and insecurity. We all will. Preparing for these times can mean the difference between giving up and persevering. It would be naive to think that you are going to be able to go into life with the same amount of energy and determination day in and day out. So, if you can think ahead to any possible obstacles that might arise, you'll be one step ahead of the game. If you factor in time for potential downfalls and days when things will not be going your way, you're less likely to feel crushed or disoriented when they arise.

Remember that there will always be times when things take a dip. There will be days when you just feel low and can't seem to get yourself moving, and this is when you will be tested the most. It's easy to give up after falling at a hurdle. But in these moments, it's imperative that you keep the end reward at the forefront of your mind. Take time to rest and brush yourself off. Cry your tears, live your anger. Then get up, forgive yourself, and move past it. Most of the things we want in life, must be worked for. Many things will require patience and resilience. All will require self-love and self-respect.

When we think about budgeting our time, we may forget to factor in time for unplanned events. Imagine you want to spend forty hours a week working towards setting up a new business. You only want to work daytime hours from Monday to Friday because you have a part-time job on evenings and weekends. You think you can get it all done in two months or less but you forget to budget in time for the unexpected.

The first week, your dog gets sick and it takes two hours getting him to the vet and back, plus you'll probably spend an extra three hours worrying. Your focus will probably be compromised. The second week your mother calls and keeps you on the phone for an hour and a half. The third week you forgot to schedule in time to run your errands and you lose a whole day grocery shopping and getting your hair done. The fourth week you end up getting into a fender bender and suffering with neck pain and headaches for three days. The fifth week, your child has a birthday and you'll need time to buy presents and organize a party. So at the end of it all, your forty hour weeks are reduced to an average of about twenty hours due to the simple fact that life continues to go on no matter what you're working towards. Having the foresight to budget your time wisely while leaving room for difficult days and forgotten duties means that you will be more realistic with your intentions and more kind to yourself when things derail from your original plans.

The bottom line is: slow and steady wins the race. Budget your time, budget your energy, and budget your motivation. Be honest with yourself about timelines. Be honest with yourself about possible moments of defeat. Dedicate yourself to getting the life that you want no matter how many times life knocks you down. Don't use setbacks as a means for self-abuse.

Making Real and True Progress

Here's a quick recap of what we've covered in this chapter. Refer to it when you need to be reminded of what you want and how to get it.

1 - Don't settle for less.
When you settle for less, you are telling yourself that you are neither capable nor deserving of getting the things you really want out of life. You are holding yourself back when you need to be propelling yourself forward. Persevering means valuing your own happiness and giving yourself the chance to achieve all that you desire. Taking the time to embark on some honest self-reflection and personal analysis is a great way to learn about your negative habits so that you can work around them when the time comes. None of us ever have to settle for less in life, and you are no exception.

2 - Use your achievements for motivation.
Take the time to recognize your achievements, no matter how small. No matter how silly it may feel to pat yourself on the back every

time you stay on track, doing so means boosting your energy and offering yourself the respect and extra motivation it takes to move onto the next step. Practice finding the positive amidst the negative. Practice giving yourself credit for every step you take on your journey. This is an exercise in loving yourself and maintaining your motivation by tapping into the resources within. When you're feeling low, take some time to think about your accomplishments. Write down five or ten times that you overcame an obstacle and stuck to your guns. Use those past triumphs as food for your soul. Use them to reclaim your youthful vitality.

3 - Don't become distracted by less important tasks.
Sometimes you will have to be firm with yourself in order to resist the temptation to do other things when you're feeling low in your resolve. Distractions lead to procrastination, which in turn, leads to giving up. Self-discipline must come from the *self*. Do everything you can to avoid distraction. If you're tempted to do the dishes instead of working, move away from the kitchen. If you're tempted to organize your kitchen cupboards instead of going to the gym, don't let yourself. The more you practice ignoring distractions, the easier it will become.

4 - Do everything you can do TODAY.
Why wait until tomorrow if you really want to make a change? The more we put things off, the less likely we are to actually complete them. There is no point in talking about what you want to do today when you could just get stuck in right now. There is no point in obsessively planning what you're going to do if you're actually just holding yourself back from getting started. The best time to become self-disciplined is always *today*. Prove to yourself that you can and will achieve what you want by getting started ASAP. Value yourself and your dreams enough to stamp out procrastination.

5 - Get perspective on time.
Remember that the things that are going to take a while to achieve, will require more dedication than the things you can accomplish in a day or a week. When you are able to realistically view the time it will take to accomplish your goal in the context of your life, you are less likely to give up when the days seem long. What is a year in the

course of your whole life? Maintaining perspective on time, rather than allowing yourself to blow things out of proportion, is a valuable tool to have on your side when you're reaching for something that will take a while to achieve.

6 - Stop making excuses.

If you have a tendency to place the blame on external factors when things don't go your way, you will find excuses to give up on virtually anything. The sooner you own up to that tendency, the better. It is okay to make mistakes and it is common to self sabotage from time to time, but the more you fess up to that, the more likely you will be to break that bad habit. If you know that you are prone to making excuses, don't beat yourself up about it. Just bear it in mind as you move forward. When you make excuses, it can make you feel better about your failures in the short term. But in the long run, doing so could gradually chip away at your self-esteem and hold you back from achieving virtually anything.

7 - Think in terms of consequence and reward.

This will help you better avoid mistakes and setbacks. If you feel your energy waning, remember *why* you're doing what you're doing. Remember that instant gratification is a temporary thing. If you keep your end goal in mind and try to keep it fresh, you will have a stronger resolve when things are difficult. It's common to feel impatient about goals that are likely to take a long time to reach. Try to keep yourself excited about your goal by talking about it periodically and thinking about why you started in the first place. Self discipline is tested the most when you have to maintain it long term, so do everything you can to keep plenty of rewards in sight. When you are tempted to go in a different direction, think about the consequence that might have on your future.

8 - Tap into your resources.

If there is someone you know that is great at staying motivated, ask them for some guidance when you're stumped or when need a confidence boost. If there is someone you can ask for help, get them on board. A friend who has great organizational skills might be able to offer you some tips and tricks that will help you stay on task. A family member who has the skills you desire, might be a helpful resource when you get stuck at a hurdle. Remember also, to use your past experiences as learning tools as well. We can all achieve more by worrying less about our pride and focusing more on doing everything we can to get the job done, and that includes thinking productively about our pasts.

9 - Think about what you're giving yourself.
Don't focus on the things you're keeping from yourself. The way we think has a lot of power over how we behave. If you constantly think of all the things you "can't" have, you will never fully appreciate the things that you can and do have. The desire for what you can't have could easily override your best intentions and lead you down a destructive path. It takes practice to rewire our thinking but having a positive mental attitude will always help, no matter what you're facing.

10 - Leave room for inevitable moments of uncertainty.
Factor in time for when things won't necessarily be going your way. It would be naive to assume that you're always going to wake up feeling great. Similarly, if we ignore the fact that sometimes the unexpected will happen, we are likely to be more easily thrown off course when it does. Leaving room for the possibility that you will have bad days somewhere along your journey means that you will be better equipped to take them in your stride. Remember, there is no square one in self-progression. The work you put in is always there no matter what overshadows it. The only direction in self-progression is forward. Your hard work cannot be undone. It will always be valid. It will always be something to feel good about. There will always be hiccups and moments when things will reach a stand still, but backwards does not exist.

"It does not matter how slowly you go as long as you do not stop."
Confucius

Coping With Failure

"Failure is simply the opportunity to begin again, this time more intelligently."
Henry Ford

When it comes to self-discipline, many people tend to ignore or underestimate the possibility for failure and how it could affect them. Most of us will face failures here and there as our lives progress, and some of us will face more than others. It could be said that failure has the ability to make or break us. Failing could lead us to give up on ourselves, or it could strengthen our resolve and feed our determination. These responses depend not just on the type of person you are, but also on what other things are going on in your life at the time. Similarly, failing at something you've worked towards you whole life will obviously hurt more than something less significant. So much of what happens in life is out of our control and this is an important factor to keep in mind. Sometimes things just don't go our way.

But other times, for whatever reason, we just don't live up to our potential. It's easy for us to get knocked down. When we're tired or stressed, our performance will suffer. When life is tumultuous, our potential for failure will be heightened. But it's not failure itself that we should fear. Rather, it's how we respond to failure - what we *do* with it - that determines whether or not we will get up and try again.

You have to remember that life can be thought of as simply a series of choices. Your whole life is a choice. What you do in a single day involves choices and what you do with your life in the long run also boils down to choices. Whatever it is that you're working towards, you get to choose the end result to some degree. You get to choose how triumph affects you and how failure affects you. A lot of times, you will get to choose between the easy road and the hard road. The easy road is tempting because it's shorter, less challenging, and offers less chance for failure. But the reward at the end of the easy road is unlikely to be anything to write home about.

Conversely, the hard road has ups and downs, twists and turns, and a higher potential for emotional bumps and bruises. It will leave you feeling challenged, exhausted at times, scared of the future, terrified of failure… but the reward at the end of this road is abundant. It offers positivity, achievement, satisfaction, pride, higher self-esteem, stronger self-beliefs, personal gratification and overall contentment with life. The end result when you persevere down the hard road well exceeds the instant gratification (and subsequent low spirits) you might get from taking the easy road or giving up.

Choices like this are complex and there is usually a lot of weigh out in order to make an informed decision about what's right for you. Are the potential rewards worth the potential pitfalls? What will you feel like at the end of either of these two roads? Can you harness the bravery you'll need to take a journey down the hard road? Are your systems a bit too depleted for that journey right now? Taking time to weigh these things out within the confines of your life as it stands today, is immensely important. If you're in a period of low mood or things at home or at work aren't great right now, you might be better off taking the easy road for now. Then you'll be able to use the reward at the end of that road to build your self-confidence and encourage you to take the next step. If things in your life are under control right now and easily manageable, maybe now would be a good time to dive into the deep end. At the end of the day, the choice is important, but it's your call.

Whatever road you end up taking, failure is always possible. It happens to the best of us. It should come as no great surprise that failure can affect, or even define, how we feel about ourselves. It can shape the way we view ourselves among our peers and the world around us. It can make us cynical or bitter. It can make us timid and afraid. But if we're going to get anywhere in life we have to develop a thicker skin. We have to be resilient. We can't let ourselves be defined by our shortcomings. We need the strength to learn from our mistakes and the courage try again. The real successes in life aren't the ones that are easily achieved. On the contrary, the real successes in life are those that occur after we've been knocked down. *Success* is every single time we get back up start again. *Success* is achieving something even after we've failed at it. *Success* is being able to trust and believe in yourself.

Your self-esteem is highly dependent on how you cope with failure. If you use failure as a stick to beat yourself with, getting up and trying again mightn't be possible at all. If you let failure determine how you feel about yourself, you'll never have the strength to persevere when times get tough again. The thing is, confidence and self-esteem are vital components of success. Ignoring this element could mean giving in to patterns of decreased motivation, low-energy attempts at change, and being unnecessarily hard on yourself. You have to be able to forgive yourself when you fail. You cannot allow the bumps and bruises of the hard road to trick you into believing that you can't get what you want. *Knowing* that you deserve more, makes getting it significantly easier. This is why loving yourself and wanting the best for yourself is so important. Being able to withstand the slap of failure and keep your head held high in times of weakness and doubt will always lead you to greater things.

Many of us are sensitive individuals. We may have had difficult childhoods, unsatisfying adulthoods, or suffered more hardships than most. Others are simply sensitive by nature. But being sensitive could mean feeling the effects of failure with brute force. In these instances, self-acceptance may be difficult to muster up. But as with so many other things I've discussed thus far, we need to be able to get perspective in order to carry on. We have to believe and accept that failure is a part of everyone's life. Failing does not mean that you are weak or that you deserve any less than other people. Failing simply means that you are a human being who is reaching for a better life. How could you possibly feel bad about that? There is nothing wrong with being sensitive or emotional. These feelings are merely proof of your humanity. If we allow failure to convince us that we are not worthy of what we're working toward - if we allow it to hold us back from taking risks - we aren't living.

Many of us give up after failing because it's too hard to endure the possibility of failing again. But by keeping it in perspective, by thinking of failure as an inevitable occurrence that will strike throughout our lives, we will naturally be more prepared and more resilient when it does. Think of failure like a hurricane. It can make life difficult, it can cause us to change our course, it can even have the force to destroy virtually everything we have. But what do we do after a hurricane? Does the entire population of a city just wander aimlessly into the next town and hope for the best? Or do we gather up what belongings we still possess and start rebuilding? How many cities have been destroyed by hurricanes yet have found the courage to get back on their feet again?

When things don't go the way you planned, you're allowed to take some time to lick your wounds. It is only natural to feel disappointed, embarrassed, or afraid. It makes sense that you'll feel a bit low. And you might need to take a day, a night, or a week to allow yourself to feel your sadness. But then, you've got to find the encouragement beneath the discouragement. When morning comes, you have to push yourself to get back on your feet and lift your chin again. This is the moment that you will need to be at your strongest. And it is this moment that determines what's going to happen next. If you stay strong in your resolve - even if you're afraid or a little under-confident - you are proving to yourself that you can accomplish what you want.

You *can* do this. It is how you cope with a fall that determines how you feel about yourself. Rise up and your confidence and self-esteem will benefit. Give up and your confidence will lower; your self-esteem will become less stable.

It is better to fail at something you've put your heart and soul into than it is to fail at something you gave up on. I believe this because *knowing* that you can stick with something through thick and thin, forms stronger self-beliefs. It may hurt worse on an emotional level, but being able to identify what you need to do differently the next time, means that you have learned from your mistakes. Therefore, you have actually gained something from your attempt rather than letting it be a total loss. When you fail while trying, you can keep your head held high. You can feel good about the fact that you didn't give up. But if you fail by giving up, you will have gained little other than the belief that you can't have what you're working towards; that you're not good enough.

Every time you get back up and try again, you believe in yourself. You are being your own cheerleader. You are creating positive habits. You are presenting yourself with an opportunity and letting yourself reach for more. It is these moments that build strength of character. These are the moments that you will be proud of later. These are the moments when people will look up to you the most.

I mentioned in the last chapter that n our minds, most of us have a nagging, negative voice that creeps in when times are tough. This is the voice that kicks us when we're down. It's the voice that tells us to give up; the voice that tells us we're not good enough. It reminds us of our shortcomings, it taunts us. For some people this may be the voice of a disproving parent, teacher, or peer from their earlier life. For others, it will simply be their own defeated voice reminding them of past failures, telling them that there's nothing to do but give up. You have to be able to recognize when that voice kicks in and starts nagging you with negativity. You have to be able to silence it and replace it with a voice of understanding, compassion, and encouragement. This will take practice and patience.

Good habits can be the hardest habits to form. But, failure rules the kingdom of negative self-beliefs. And if we cannot accept our failures and bounce back from them, they will seep into our core and rewrite the way we think of ourselves. The more afraid of failure you are, the less likely you will be to succeed. Therefore, by giving yourself room for setbacks, by giving yourself the permission to shrug off your failures and move on, you are strengthening your resolve and allowing yourself the freedom to rise above them. Failures are experiences that we can all learn and grow from if we use them the right way.

At the beginning of this book, I told you that you will have to believe in yourself if you want to become more self-disciplined. Each time you get back up after a failure, you are providing yourself with that self-belief. Each time you prove to yourself that you can get up and fight again; that you are resilient, steadfast, and strong;

you are believing in yourself. No amount of organization, time management, or vision boards can replace this vital ingredient of self-discipline. So think of failure as fuel. Use it to motivate you. Use it to lift yourself up. Accept it and rise above it.

Failure and Starting Again

Here is a list of everything you've learned in this chapter. Refer to it anytime failure features in your life; whether you have failed or you're facing the potential to fail.

1 - Failure is inevitable to some extent.
It happens to everyone; some, more than others. We have to accept and expect that failure will feature in our lives at some point or another. But failure can make or break you, so what you do with it is far more important than failure itself. Rather than letting failure bring you down, use it to strengthen your resolve. It takes courage to take risks and doing so should be celebrated no matter what gets in your way. As you move through life, leave room for all possibilities. We cannot predict exactly what will happen on our journeys, so it's wise to keep an open mind about all potentialities.

2 - Life is a choice.
And though much of what happens in our lives is out of our control, we have to be able to recognize what choices we do have. You can choose to succeed by facing the possibility for failure and forging ahead anyway. You get to choose between taking the easy road or fighting your way down the hard road, and there is no right or wrong answer where this is concerned. There is no formula that will work for everyone. As long as you make informed decisions based on yourself and your life as it stands, you will continue to move in the right direction.

3 - Don't define yourself by your failures.
We cannot judge ourselves by our failures alone. Doing so would be detrimental to our self worth. Think more about how you cope with failure. We need to use our failures to advantage. We need to learn

from them, write some new plans, get back up and carry on. Because that's where true success lies. Success isn't just the end goal you have in mind, it's how to conduct yourself as you move from one point to another.

4 - It's okay to be sensitive.

We are all unique individuals and for some of us, failing can really hurt. It can seem like a total catastrophe or it could send us plummeting into depression or feelings of low self worth. But you have to remember that being sad and disappointed is only natural after a failure. It doesn't mean that you're weak or that you are less worthy of what you're reaching for. Crying or feeling anxious about the future doesn't mean that you're not strong enough to try again. Emotions are not something to be afraid of. They are not something to be scared of or to beat ourselves up over. They are our most basic, natural responses to the ups and downs we face in life. But at the end of the day, when the hurricane has passed, we have to be able to get back up and start rebuilding. We are all strong enough to do that, even if we don't feel like it at the time. Failure builds strength and knowledge and those are two fantastic things to have on your side.

5 - It is better to fail trying.

It may hurt to fail at something you've been working at for a long time, but at the end of the day, it's better to know that you put up a good fight than it is to know that you gave up. When you fail trying, you reiterate your positive self-beliefs. You're proving to yourself that you can push through times that are challenging. These are times when you should feel proud. As you move toward challenges in life, make sure to give yourself room for setbacks. Remember that the road is not always easy and things rarely go exactly as we've planned. Forgive yourself for your failures. Nurture and love yourself. Let your inner voice be one of compassion and understanding.

"Each mistake teaches you something new about yourself. There is no failure, remember, except in no longer trying. It is the courage to continue that counts."
Chris Bradford

Be The Phoenix

"The most difficult thing is the decision to act, the rest is merely tenacity."
Ameila Earhart

Self-discipline and getting what you want out of life are very closely linked. One will almost never exist without the other. Self-discipline is both a skill and a frame of mind. It is an intricate lacing of practical skills and having control over your self-beliefs in as well as your beliefs about the world around you. You do not have to be the strongest person in the world to be self-disciplined. You do not need to have wealth or good fortune in order to achieve what you'd like. No matter what life has been like for you up to this point, change is possible. You can always become stronger. You can always start again. You can always climb up out of the rubble and learn to fly. Whether you'd like to improve a few small things or cut out a whole new life for yourself, *you can.*

Perseverance takes practice, and without it, very few of us will achieve the level of self-discipline we desire. But all of the things you learn throughout life are valuable to your future. Everything that happens in your life can be used to help shape your coming days. This encompasses everything from how you cope with failure to how you organize your schedule. When you find something that works for you, carry that with you into your future ventures. When you try something that doesn't work, let it fall by the wayside and try something else. There is no cookie cutter method to ensure greater self-discipline. You've got to work with what you've got. You have to learn to find the good amongst the bad. You have to be able to learn from your mistakes *and* your triumphs.

You have to practice keeping your chin up and getting out of bed even when you don't want to. But most importantly, you have to look at your accomplishments with pride. You have to be able to reflect on your hard work and use it as a tool to increase your motivation and keep your head up when the going gets tough. Everything you have accomplished in life is a resource that you can use to shed light on what systems work best for you. Everything you've lived through can tell you something about your instincts, behaviors, strengths and weaknesses. They are resources that can guide you through each step you take in life.

In order to go into new projects with the best possible outcome, take time to reflect on your past experiences regularly. Self-reflection can have astounding effects on how we cope with life. Think about the times you failed and really try to figure out what went wrong. This could mean anything from dropping out of college to simply having an unsuccessful conversation with a friend. Think about what happened and what you could've done better. Whatever it is, forgive yourself for that mistake and make a vow to try not to do it again. Think about the times you have succeeded and explore what it was that kept you on track.

Would it help you to get the opinion of a friend when you're struggling? Do you think you could rearrange your schedule to better suit the thing you're attempting to conquer? Do you need to pare down the amount of things you're trying to do at once so that you'll get more done in the long run? Could you benefit from trying out a new app to block distracting websites when you're working or studying? Do you need to tell your family that you will not be keeping junk food in the house because you need to make things easier on yourself?

It is okay to ask for that type of support from your loved ones. It is always okay to reach out to the people that love you for guidance and support. If you make excuses for your shortcomings a lot, maybe it's time to get real and be honest with yourself about it. By making excuses are you holding yourself back? Are you self-sabotaging? Is it possible that you don't actually want the thing you're reaching for but that you're doing it to make someone else happy? Might you need to reevaluate some of the relationships in your life? How can you do things better next time?

Getting used to reflecting on your experiences and asking yourself questions like this is a valuable skill to have on your side throughout life. When we speak to ourselves this way, we are giving ourselves the opportunity to think more deeply about our feelings and actions. This, in turn, will help us better understand our feelings, instincts, and behavior. It will help us understand why we feel the way we do when things don't go our way. It will help us to maintain our relationships in every aspect of life. More importantly, it will help us identify our weaknesses, therefore, giving us the power to strengthen them.

No one can force you to stay on track like you can. You are the one that has to ignore the distractions when it's time to get to work. You are the one that has to avoid the mistakes and setbacks, to say no to cake when you want to lose weight, to say no to cigarettes when you want better health. You are the one who has to ignore the sink full of dishes when you need to focus on work instead. You are the one who has to work hard to reach your financial goals or to get that degree you've always wanted. No one else can do these things for you. No one else has the power to give it all to you or to take it all away from you. That is why it's called *self*-discipline.

An alarm clock may ring but it will not pick you up out of bed. An appointment may exist but your legs have to carry you there. Your friends can offer their support, but they cannot do the work for you. This is why you have to believe in yourself. This is why you have to be steadfast in your goals, why you have to persevere when things get hard, why you have to dust yourself off after a failure and get back up. Because in the end, it's *you* that either reaches the goal or doesn't. It's you that gets the reward or faces the consequence.

No matter who you are or what your life has been like up to now, change is possible. You can be Richie Rich or Oliver Twist and still get more out of life. You can always be more tomorrow than you are today. You can have the life you want and do the things you want to do. You just have to be careful not to stand in your own way. You have to recognize if you're spending more time planning than doing. You have to recognize when you're putting yourself down rather than lifting yourself up. You have to recognize when you're procrastinating and STOP.

You have to recognize when you're giving in to self-doubt and STOP. The Tough Love Approach isn't always enjoyable but it's a great way to get things done. Setting challenges for yourself is character building. Working hard is confidence building. One of the greatest gifts of being human is our ability to grow and change throughout our time on earth. Why would we ever waste that?

Bring all your energy. Bring all your might. You've got this.

When you embark on a journey - be it a journey of the self or of the world - you have to remember that your past does not have to define your future. We can use our past experiences to either hold us back or to guide us forward. We can choose to forget about the negative stuff and cling to the positive if we want to. If life has been hard on you, you might need to fight a little bit harder to get what you want. You might have to start by changing the way you think about yourself. You might need to heal first or explore the way you feel about your identity. You might need to finally let go of the things that have held you down in life so that you can be free to enjoy lightness in the future.

The thing is, none of us are perfect. We all feel fear and trepidation. We all make mistakes. We all go through losses and failures. And most of us want more than what we have today. We want to be better versions of ourselves. But in order for us to do so, we have to believe in ourselves. We have to be strict with ourselves. We have to set rules that we will actually abide by. We have to stop comparing ourselves to other people.

When it comes to self-discipline, you have to start by being willing to take a chance on yourself. That means being willing to forgive yourself when things go wrong. It means being prepared to celebrate each step along the way. You have to make a promise to yourself that you will keep. Promise yourself that you will not give up. Promise that you will be kind to yourself when things are difficult. Promise that you will get what you want out of life no matter what.

Marry yourself to the idea. Then, keep these promises in your thoughts when you are faced with adversity. Don't let setbacks steal your resolve. Remember not to beat yourself up when things don't go your way. Instead, summon up your compassionate, encouraging inner voice and silence the nagging negative voice. Stick to your guns. If you find a system that works for you, don't waver from it. If you need help, ask for it. Use every resource you have.

Bring all your energy. Bring all your might. You've got this.

47592130R00044

Made in the USA
Middletown, DE
08 June 2019